Introduction

While visiting the Sussex village of Burwash on a summer's day in 190[ ] writer Rudyard Kipling set his hea[ ] nearby Jacobean house called Bateman's. Two years later he completed the purchase and settled into the house that he would make his home for the rest of his life. Kipling died in 1936 and ever since then his literary reputation has divided opinion, but it is clear from many of his writings that Sussex became his adopted home and affected him deeply. At about the time Kipling moved into Bateman's, he wrote the poem *Sussex*. For anyone today standing on the crest of the downs that lie between Lewes and Eastbourne or on the sea cliffs that stretch eastwards from Hastings towards Rye, the series of images evoked in Kipling's poem can read not so much like a list of locations to be visited but rather a litany of sacred places to be revered.

With his poetic eye, Kipling conjures up Sussex's 'fair ground', far from Baltic pines and palm groves, far even from Surrey glades. What he loves about Sussex is a surprising promise of wildness and perspective – the chasing shadows on the whale-backed downs, the gnarled and writhen thorn, the Channel's leaden line. He imagines the signs of past inhabitants – the barrows and camps and old gods of a heathen kingdom. Others, Kipling surmises, may prefer the places and English counties that lie from the Thames to the Tweed, but for him there is

Kipling was born in India, sent to Britain to be educated and then returned to India for his early life as an adult. When first married, he also lived for a number of years in the United States. By the time he arrived at Bateman's Kipling was in search of a more settled, peaceful life. Near the end of the poem comes his expression of hope that if we can but give our hearts to the land, even to just one small spot of earth, then something magical happens and its effects can be beyond the limits of speech and thought and reason. Kipling came across his 'earth to love' unexpectedly and, as he describes in the poem, it fell to him by lot on the bare slopes of the downs, along the white cliff edges, in the woods of the Weald, beside the wide-banked Ouse, among the shaws and deep ghylls and under the rolled scarp. In whichever of these places Kipling found himself, he experienced a simple and profound joy, shared by many since, in his beloved 'Sussex by the sea'.

About this guide
This guide contains 40 routes ranging in length from an hour's stroll to a day's walking, divided into five sections broadly based on the topography of the county. Most of the routes are circular and are intended as comfortable walks or strolls. On some routes the cumulative ascent or

some steeper escarpments of the downs may require greater exertion than the strict route length suggests, but in general the walking is on well-worn paths, lanes and tracks, with plenty of waymarks, which should require minimal time and effort for route-finding. The route descriptions concentrate on the salient points of navigation, but may not cover every twist or turn. If in doubt, the obvious path is usually the line to take. In addition, the accompanying sketch maps serve an illustrative purpose and, for the longer or more complex routes, it would be a good idea to have access to the relevant OS Explorer mapping, details of which are given at the start of each walk.

The recommended time for each walk is an estimate based on an average walking speed of 4kmph, with a small allowance added in on some hillier or clifftop routes. However, timings will vary significantly, not only for individuals but also given the seasonal effects on paths, especially those crossing fields, or tracks on the downs, sections of which can become muddier and more slippery at certain times of year. A few routes also pass along cliff edges, tidal rivers or sections of coastline which can become inaccessible depending on the state of the tide. Most paths covered in the routes are well-used and well-maintained by local agencies but, in spring and summer especially, hedges and undergrowth grow vigorously and nettles, brambles and

thorn can infiltrate narrower paths, stile crossings and gates. Signage of rights of way in East Sussex is generally very good, especially on waymarked routes such as the South Downs Way, the England Coast Path, the Wealdway, and the 1066 Country Walk.

It is hoped that there is plenty of interest along the routes themselves and it would be possible to spread a short walk over half a day if time is taken to explore along the way. Conversely, some of the routes are short enough to attempt two in a day. In addition, this volume's companion *West Sussex: 40 Coast and Country Walks* provides further scope for exploring the region on foot.

Getting around and access

Many of the towns in East Sussex can serve as useful bases for walking. In the north of the county, the main towns are Crowborough, Uckfield and Heathfield, while East Grinstead and Royal Tunbridge Wells are within easy reach, just over the county border in neighbouring West Sussex and Kent. The county town of Lewes is the gateway to the section of the South Downs that runs eastwards from Brighton to Eastbourne, which itself is also well-placed for exploring the coast and Pevensey Levels. Finally, the towns of Hastings, Battle and Rye provide an historic setting for discovering the easternmost part of the county.

There are no motorways in East Sussex

and the major routes of the A21, A22 and A27 can become very busy at peak times and during holidays. A good number of the main towns have railway stations, with mainline routes from London to Lewes and Hastings, as well as a regular service along the south coast between Brighton and Rye. Regular bus routes serve the main towns and, in particular, several services along the south coast are useful for walkers. An effort has been made to start walks from places which are served by public transport and, in addition, it would usually be possible to plan the completion of a walk from a town to coincide with train times. It is worth noting that it is increasingly the case that many villages in rural areas are only intermittently served by public bus on a weekly or seasonal basis. Access by car is still the preferred option for many and, while towns cater adequately for parking, this can be a sensitive issue in smaller villages and hamlets. Pubs and

inns can be very accommodating if the intention is to visit before or after a walk, but where parking is outside designated car parks consideration should be shown for the needs and access of local residents and the farming community.

East Sussex is still substantially a rural county and has traditionally been associated with mixed farming, including fruit orchards and now vineyards, and in some areas sheep, arable and dairy farming can all be encountered in the space of a single walk. At lambing time, signs on gates may well request that dogs are kept on leads and the presence of dogs for cows can be problematic – it is not unheard of for cows with calves to behave in a very protective way. Even without a dog, cattle just released from winter shelters or cows which have recently calved should be left well alone. If in doubt, it is usually advisable and possible to find a short detour to avoid such livestock.

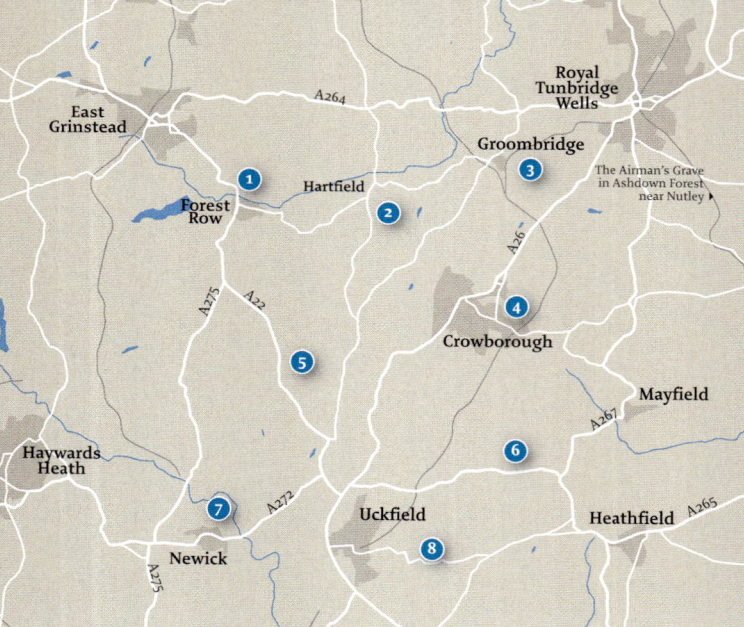

The Airman's Grave
in Ashdown Forest
near Nutley ▶

The northwestern corner of East Sussex is dominated by the high heathland of Ashdown Forest, which rises to more than 200m and gives expansive views out over the Weald to the South Downs. Being a relatively short distance from London and the conurbations of Kent and Surrey, the area has become ever more popular in recent years, especially on summer weekends. On Ashdown's northern edge you will find the infant River Medway and beyond that a patchwork of fields and old farms, while devotees of Winnie-the-Pooh are regularly drawn to Five Hundred Acre Wood near Hartfield and other locations associated with A A Milne's stories of Christopher Robin and friends. Further east, the sandstone outcrops of Harrison's Rocks and Eridge Rocks near Groombridge are one of the most visited locations for climbing in the South East. Watching the climbers' moves and listening to their calls can add an entertaining dimension to a country walk. Crowborough is the main town on the Forest's eastern fringe and just a short distance from the town's railway station is the hidden dell of The Ghyll, a wooded nature reserve. The ground to the south gradually dips down to the woods of the Sussex Weald and the Ouse Valley and provides some gentle walking.

Crowborough and Ashdown Forest

Forest Row

Distance 9km **Time** 2 hours 30
Terrain fields and woods on well-
waymarked bridleways and lanes
Map OS Explorer 135 **Access** bus to Forest
Row from Uckfield and East Grinstead
(stops on Hartfield Rd near Station Rd)

**Explore the less visited wooded folds
and fields of the Wealden countryside
that lie to the north of Ashdown Forest
and the River Medway.**

The walk starts from the large village
of Forest Row, where there are a number
of cafés, pubs and teashops, as well as a
handy council car park along Hartfield
Road. The village, as the name suggests,
has a long association with Ashdown
Forest to the south and through it flows
the upper reach of the infant River
Medway, whose source is not far away
over the county border in West Sussex.

From the centre of Forest Row by the

church, head down Hartfield Road and
turn left along Station Road, along which
you cross the River Medway. At the end of
the road, continue ahead with the
Vanguard Way through the private parking
area and cross the former railway line. The
Vanguard Way, which is followed for the
first half of the route, now heads past the
pumping station and up the edge of the
field beyond. From here, it continues for
the next 1km uphill on a fenced and
wooded path over the top of the hill to
Cansiron Lane.

Turn left down the rough lane for 200m
to Grove Farm Cottages and, at the bend
beyond, make sure you turn right off the
lane. The Vanguard Way continues along
the private lane to the entrance to Great
Surries and doglegs left for 75m to the
next junction, where it turns right. After
400m, you pass the imposing stone façade
of Thornhill and continue down the

◄ Dog Gate Lodge above Owlett's Farm

winding lane for just over 1km to the bend at Dog Gate Lodge.

Leave the Vanguard Way here to bend right with the lane heading steeply down to Owlett's Farm and past the buildings to a gate at the bottom. The route now continues ahead uphill along the hedged bridleway, which soon bends right and then passes alongside Holden Wood to a bridleway junction. Bear right and follow the bridleway for the next 1km up through the trees, over the rise and between fields to the junction with Cansiron Lane by the communications mast.

Turn right along the rough lane and, after 400m where the lane bends a little right, look out for a stile on the left. Cross the stile onto the route of the High Weald Landscape Trail. Follow the waymarks down through the wood and over a crosspaths to a T-junction. The Landscape Trail turns left and at the end of the wood forks right down the edge of two fields to a track. Turn right along the track and follow it downhill to the lane by Tablehurst Farm. Here, dogleg right up the lane for 100m, then left down a walkway to the former railway line, which carries the Forest Way and the National Route 21 cyclepath. Cross over onto the bridleway signed for Forest Row which crosses a footbridge, heads along a field and then bears right to Station Road. From here, retrace your steps up to the centre of Forest Row.

9

Hartfield and Five Hundred Acre Wood

Distance 10km **Time** 2 hours 45
Terrain fields, lanes and woodland
Map OS Explorer 135 **Access** bus to
Hartfield from Crawley and
Royal Tunbridge Wells

**This walk rambles through countryside
on the northern edge of Ashdown Forest,
a setting which inspired A A Milne to
write the stories of Winnie-the-Pooh.**

The walk starts from the village of
Hartfield, where there is parking on the
roadside and, during weekends and
school holidays, in the car park off the
High Street by the primary school.

From the centre of the village, head up
Church Street past cottages and, opposite
St Mary's Church, turn right over a stile
into fields with the High Weald Landscape
Trail. Follow the left-hand edge of the first
two fields, then head across the third field
down to its bottom left corner and over a
stream. Walk along the edge of a fourth

field past Forstal Farm to a track. Turn left
onto the track over the stream, then go
immediately left again onto a footpath,
which leads up through woodland to its
far edge, and cross a fifth field to the
Buckhurst Estate road.

Turn right onto the route of the
Wealdway and head up the estate road for
the next 1.6km past a cottage, Thatchers,
down across a dip and up past a row of
cottages to the entrance to Fisher's Gate.
Bear left over a stile here and walk down
along the field edge, then bend right up to
a junction of estate roads just inside Five
Hundred Acre Wood.

Turn left off the Wealdway and follow
the footpath along the estate road at the
northern edge of the wood for just over
800m down to the B2188. Turn left for
200m along this straight section of road,
where there is a narrow verge, to the
junction with Whitehouse Lane. Fork
right onto the lane and follow it down

◄ Memorials in St Michael and All Angels Church, Withyham

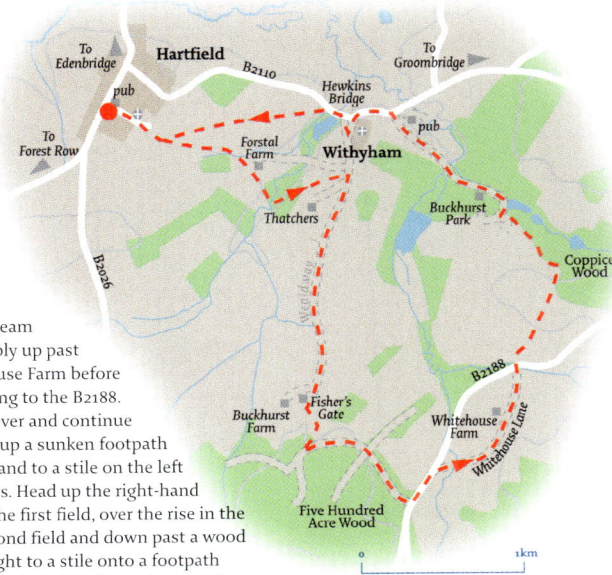

over a stream and steeply up past Whitehouse Farm before descending to the B2188.

Cross over and continue for 150m up a sunken footpath in woodland to a stile on the left into fields. Head up the right-hand edge of the first field, over the rise in the large second field and down past a wood on the right to a stile onto a footpath along a track. Go left down the track for 500m to a junction with an estate road in Buckhurst Park. Turn right down the estate road past two lakes and some cottages. Continue along the estate road over the rise and downhill to emerge on the B2110 in Withyham.

Turn left along the pavement for 200m and then continue along the raised footpath which bends left above the road to St Michael and All Angels Church and a junction with the Buckhurst Estate road.

Turn right onto the Wealdway down to the B2110 and go left along it over Hewkins Bridge. Just beyond, take the footpath off left into fields. Head up the first field to a gate and continue past a small wood over the second field. Go diagonally across the large third field and keep ahead across the top of the fourth to a stile. From here, retrace the outward route along the edges of two fields and back down Church Street.

The Rocks of Groombridge

Distance 9.5km **Time** 2 hours 45
Terrain lanes, woods and fields
Map OS Explorer 135 **Access** bus to
**Groombridge from Crawley and
Royal Tunbridge Wells**

There's plenty to see on this route past
two sandstone outcrops, popular with
climbers, and on through a woodland
nature reserve.

The walk starts from the village of
Groombridge, where there is parking off
Station Road behind the village hall in the
Wealden Council car park. Opposite the
village hall, head up Corseley Road for
500m on the route of the High Weald
Landscape Trail, which is followed for the
first half of the walk as far as Eridge
Rocks. Continue past the church and
school to the bend and turn left along a
footpath over the railway bridge, beyond
which the footpath continues for 400m
between fields to the entrance driveway
to Birchden Wood. Turn right along the
driveway for just over 100m, then fork left
down through the trees. Continue over a
track, past the car park, where there are
public toilets, and out of the wood.

The footpath soon bends left and heads
alongside the railway line with Harrison's
Rocks over to the left. Follow the footpath
around the southern end of the crags,
past cottages and Forge Farmhouse. The
footpath continues to bear round to the
left and heads uphill out of the woods
and between fields to Pinstraw Farm.
Continue up the rough lane to Eridge
Road at Park Corner.

Turn right for 250m down the road past
Normans Cottage to the bend. Just round
the bend turn left with the High Weald
Landscape Trail along a field edge, over
some footbridges and then up the middle
of a large field. Continue up past Warren

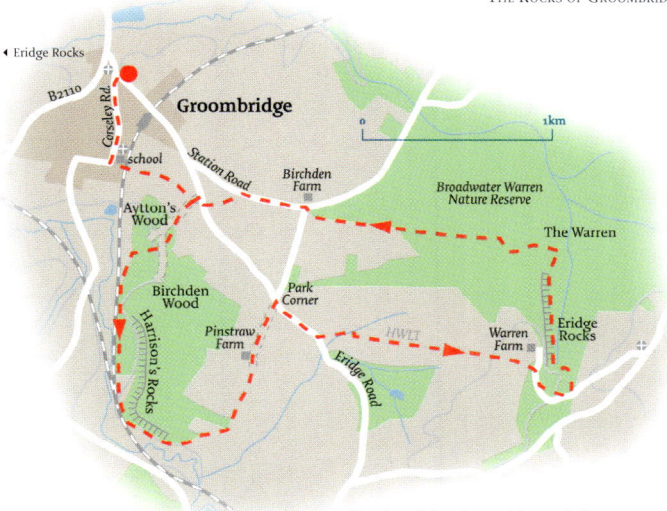

◄ Eridge Rocks

B2110

Corseley Rd.

Groombridge

school

Station Road

Birchden Farm

Broadwater Warren Nature Reserve

Aytton's Wood

The Warren

0   1km

Birchden Wood

Harrison's Rocks

Park Corner

Pinstraw Farm

HWLT

Eridge Road

Warren Farm

Eridge Rocks

Farm to Warren Farm Lane. Dogleg right for 100m along the wooded lane, then left onto a footpath through the trees down to the small car park at Eridge Rocks. The site is owned and managed by Sussex Wildlife Trust and there are a number of information panels throughout the reserve about the geology and wildlife found here.

Leave the High Weald Landscape Trail here and turn left along the path below the crags. After 150m, at a fork, bend left with the path which winds its way along the base of the crags. By the path junction at the end of the rocks, keep ahead for another 200m down to a track T-junction by a veteran oak tree.

Turn left along the forestry track for 300m to the second track on the right.

Dogleg right along this track for 100m, then left through a gate. Follow the track alongside a fence with good views over Broadwater Warren Nature Reserve. After 600m, go through a gate and, at the track junction 30m beyond, fork left onto the path along the edge of the wood for 500m to a gate onto Park Corner Lane. Turn right to the junction and then left along Station Road for 350m to a shallow right-hand bend. Here, just before the village sign for Groombridge, take the footpath off left over a field to Eridge Road. Dogleg right for 50m along the road, then left down the entrance driveway to Birchden Wood. After just 50m, turn right onto the High Weald Landscape Trail and retrace the outward route along the footpath, over the railway bridge and down Corseley Road to the centre of Groombridge.

Crowborough and The Ghyll

Distance 5.5km **Time** 1 hour 30
Terrain woodland paths and tracks
Map OS Explorer 135 **Access** train to
Crowborough from South Croydon and
Uckfield; bus to Crowborough Station
from Royal Tunbridge Wells and
Crowborough town centre

**Climb up beside a stream through a now
tranquil nature reserve before wandering
back over higher ground through woods
and along an old byway.**

The walk starts from Crowborough
Railway Station in the Jarvis Brook area of
the town. Head down Station Approach to
the junction with Crowborough Hill, the
B2100. Dogleg briefly left up the road and
right into Jarvis Brook car park. To the rear
of the car park by the long-stay section,
bear left across Jarvis Brook Recreation
Ground to Burdett Road. Cross over the
road into The Ghyll Nature Reserve. Go
through the small car park and the gate at
the far end. Bear right down across a
footbridge and turn left onto the path
alongside the stream.

The reserve is a steep-sided valley
formed during the last ice age, 12,000
years ago. It is now classed as ancient
woodland as it is thought to have had
continuous tree cover for more than
400 years, but the area has not always
been such a haven for wildlife. The
remains of old furnaces and former ponds
have been found here and are a reminder
that from Roman times until the 18th
century the abundant water and trees
were used in the production of iron. The
site may also have provided the literary
inspiration for Arthur Conan Doyle, who
lived in nearby Crowborough, and his
novel *The Lost World*, after fossilised
dinosaur footprints were found here at
the beginning of the last century.

◀ The view to Rotherfield

The path rises and falls as it makes its way uphill, sometimes beside the stream and at other times on the steep bank above it. After 800m you reach a crosspaths by a second footbridge. Keep on uphill for another 250m through Jeffery's Wood to Jubilee Meadow. Head over this field past the Silver Jubilee Recreation Ground to Green Lane, the B2157, at Steel Cross.

Turn right along the pavement uphill over the junction with Palesgate Lane. Continue for another 100m and turn right onto a footpath along a track. Head along the track past houses and farm buildings and continue for another 400m between fields to a crosspaths at the edge of Limekiln Forest. Bear slightly to the right and follow the footpath ahead for 350m alongside a fence through the middle of the woodland to a junction with an old lane. Turn right and follow the lane to a junction with a byway at the southern edge of the wood.

Turn left and follow the pleasant old byway for 500m between fields to the entrance to Lime Kiln Oast. Continue ahead down the byway for another 500m, with a view left across the valley to

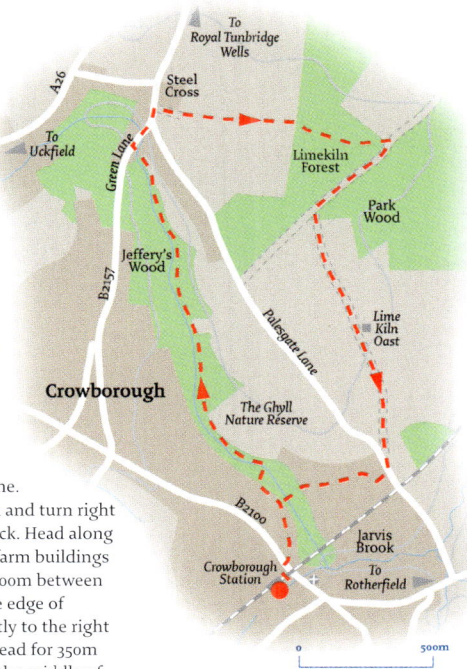

Rotherfield, to the junction with Palesgate Lane. Here, dogleg left, then almost immediately right onto a path over the grass area between the houses to Forest Rise. Bear right through the housing estate, over the rise down into Burdett Road and across The Ghyll. Here, turn left back across Jarvis Brook Recreation Ground to return to the start.

Nutley and Camp Hill

Distance 10.5km (incl short detour)
Time 3 hours 15 **Terrain** woods and
heathland, with 330m of ascent
Map OS Explorer 135 **Access** bus to Nutley
from Uckfield and East Grinstead

**Explore the extensive heathlands,
woodlands and ghyll streams of the
southern part of Ashdown Forest, one of
Europe's most important wildlife sites.**

From the centre of Nutley, head towards
the southern end of the village down the
pavement of the High Street, the A22, past
the church and turn left down Clock
House Lane. After 150m, at the fork, keep
left past houses downhill. Just past the
entrance to a house called Woodpeckers,
fork left onto a track which descends and
bends left steeply down to a stream. Head
up the far side and over the heath to a
path junction. Continue ahead and bear a
little to the left, past the entrance to

Upper Misbourne Farm – at this point the
return route comes in from the left. Go
through the gate, head down the track for
100m to the bend and fork left to stay on
the footpath down to a second stream.
Head up over the next rise and down to a
third stream and five-track junction. You
can detour left here to climb uphill for
200m to the Airman's Grave, a memorial
to the crew of a Wellington bomber which
crashed here in July 1941.

Continue ahead uphill to the top of the
rise, pass over a crosspaths and, just past
Spring Garden Farm, fork right with the
footpath up to the B2026. Cross the road
and follow the track through the trees,
gently down past a house and then more
steeply down to a stream in woodland.
Just beyond, turn left onto the Wealdway.

You now follow the waymarks of the
Wealdway to Camp Hill. The Wealdway
weaves its way northwards uphill for

◀ Ellison's Pond below Camp Hill

500m before forking right downhill and turning left along a driveway past houses. At the end of the driveway, by Browns Brook Cottage, keep ahead into the trees and over a footbridge. The Wealdway now climbs steeply up through the wood to a cottage, where the gradient eases. Keep ahead uphill to a second cottage, where the path heads left to a stile onto a rough lane. Bear right uphill along the lane for 200m and, just past some houses, keep ahead along the footpath. This takes you for another 600m over the heath and along a field edge parallel to the road to the junction with the B2026. Cross over the road and continue up to the top of Camp Hill.

On the far side of the pine trees at the track junction leave the Wealdway and turn left down the wide path to Ellison's Pond and car park beyond. Cross the road to Hollies car park and bear right along a wide path, initially parallel with the road, which curves round the head of the Misbourne Valley. Cross the shallow dip and head up the far side to a gate. Just before the gate, bear left and follow the path alongside a fence and wood downhill for 600m to a gate on the right. Go through the gate and turn immediately left down the wooded track to the crosspaths just before the entrance to Upper Misbourne Farm. Turn right back down to the first stream crossed on the outward route and retrace your steps up into Nutley.

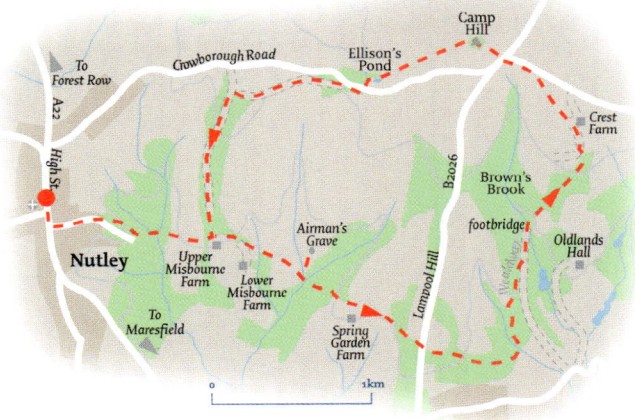

Hadlow Down

Distance 7.5km **Time** 2 hours 15 **Terrain** bridleways and footpaths through woodland and fields, winding lanes **Map** OS Explorer 135 **Access** bus to Hadlow Down from Crowborough and Uckfield (limited service, stops on A272 at Hall Lane, 200m from School Lane)

An out-of-the-way route through ancient woods and old farmsteads leads you past a mysterious moat.

The walk starts from the small village of Hadlow Down on School Lane, just off the A272 midway between Uckfield and Heathfield. Parking is available on School Lane. Walk down School Lane past the primary school. After 100m, turn left along the footpath to St Mark's Church and head around the edge of the burial ground. Cross the A272 and dogleg right along the pavement for 50m, then left onto a bridleway down a track. The bridleway heads between fields for 500m

towards Waste Wood. A little way into the trees just before the entrance to Woodlands Farm, fork right off the track. For the next 1.5km, the bridleway descends gently down through the wood before heading over a rise and down out of the trees to Warren Farm.

Continue past the buildings and farmhouse to a staggered crosspaths in woodland where the route turns right onto a footpath. A little into the wood, this descends a bank and doglegs right, then left along the edge of the wood and down past an old moat, visible over on the right. Moats are often associated with castles, forts or aristocratic residences and there are more than 6000 in England. This moated site is thought to have been constructed in the 13th century. There is no evidence of any building on the irregularly-shaped enclosure of land, which is still surrounded by a deep moat. This has

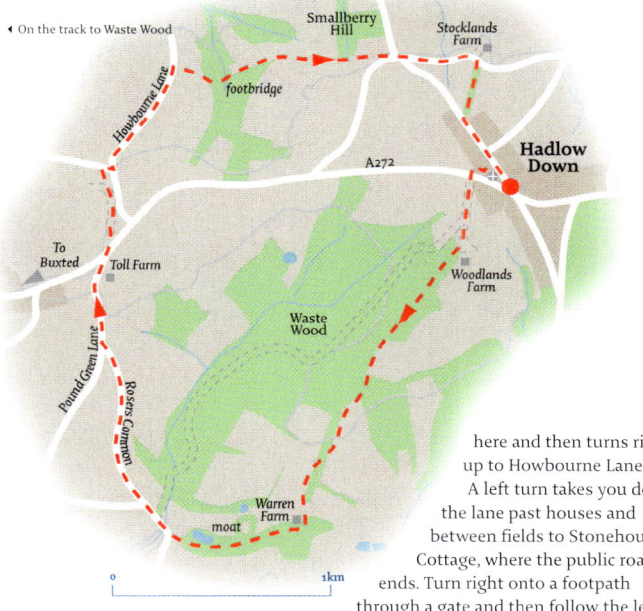

◄ On the track to Waste Wood

led archaeologists to conclude, situated as it is near Warren Farm, that it must have been used for horticultural purposes or as a protection for stock animals.

Continue along the edge of the next field, through a patch of woodland and, just before a gate, fork right over a field to a lane. The route now turns right onto the winding lane up Shepherds Hill for 1km to the junction with Pound Green Lane and then bears right for another 400m up to the A272. Cross over and follow the footpath along Spotted Cow Lane, past cottages and houses, to the end. The route forks right along a fenced passageway

here and then turns right up to Howbourne Lane.

A left turn takes you down the lane past houses and between fields to Stonehouse Cottage, where the public road ends. Turn right onto a footpath through a gate and then follow the left field edge down into woodland (this section can be a little overgrown when the bracken is high) to a gate and a footbridge beyond. Cross the footbridge, follow the footpath uphill through the wood and then bend right up a sunken way and over the rise to the driveway to Smallberry Hill.

Continue up the driveway to Five Chimneys Lane and turn left to the crossroads. Cross over and head along Stocklands Lane for 350m up to Stocklands Farm at the top of the rise. Turn right here onto the bridleway which leads uphill to School Lane, where a left turn will take you back up to the start.

Fletching and Newick

Distance 9km **Time** 2 hours 30
Terrain fields and lanes; the River Ouse is
prone to flooding **Map** OS Explorer 135
Access bus to Newick (halfway along the
route) from Uckfield, Haywards Heath
and Lewes

**Choose dry conditions for this gentle
country walk in the valley of the Upper
Ouse on the edge of Sheffield Park.**

The walk starts from the village of
Fletching, where parking is available in
the Wealden Council car park off the High
Street behind the village hall. The church
is well worth a visit and, amongst its
memorials, contains the Sheffield
Mausoleum. The historian Edward
Gibbon is also interred here, having died
in 1794 while staying with his friend, the
Earl of Sheffield, owner of nearby
Sheffield Park House, whose estate is
now managed by the National Trust as
Sheffield Park and Garden.

Walk down the High Street past the
church and round the left bend along
the road towards Piltdown. Just past
the primary school, bear right into the
recreation ground and follow its edge
round to the far corner. Head over the
small first field and follow the footpath
down beside a ditch for 250m in the
second field. Just before the woodland,
turn left up the middle of the third field,
over the rise and down to a stream. Keep
ahead up the middle of the next field,
pass to the right of the buildings and
continue up the driveway past houses
to the A272.

Cross the road and, a little to the left,
continue down a footpath along the
edges of two fields with Barkham Manor
off to the left through the trees. At the
bottom of the second field, bear left
through the hedge and head over the rise
in the next field down to Sharpsbridge
Lane. Turn right along the lane over the

◄ Looking back to the Church of St Andrew and St Mary in Fletching

River Ouse, up the hill and round the right-hand bend. Opposite the entrance to Sharpsbridge Farm, turn right up steps back into the fields.

The route now follows the right-hand edge of the fields along the top of Sharp's Hanger above the River Ouse. At the end of the second field, go through the gate and cut across the bottom of the next field. Then bear left along the edge of the fourth field. At the far end, dogleg right over a stream and then left across the bottom of the fifth field. Head up the middle of the sixth field to the churchyard. Continue past St Mary's Church and up the lane beyond to Church Road. Turn right along the pavement for 600m to The Green in Newick and head past the old pump to the pelican crossing at the A272.

Cross the road and head down the narrow lane opposite, to the left of the row of cottages and also called The Green, keeping ahead along a walled walkway between gardens up to a housing estate. Turn right along Cricketfield past some garages and then right again along Alexander Mead. At the bend, keep ahead along the track to the water treatment works and turn left into fields. Head alongside the fence and continue down to the woodland at the bottom.

Follow the footpath through the wood, across two footbridges and back into fields. Cross the first of these to a gate and then head along the edges of three more past Fletching Mill Farm. At the end of the third field, bend left past a house and through an orchard to Mill Lane. Turn right along the lane for 800m over the River Ouse and up the hill into Fletching.

Framfield and Tickerage

Distance 7.25km **Time** 2 hours
Terrain fields, lanes and woodland
Map OS Explorer OL25 **Access** bus to
Framfield from Uckfield and Heathfield

**This undulating route ambles over fields
and alongside a stream through
picturesque Wealden countryside.**

The walk starts in the centre of the
village of Framfield by the 13th-century
Church of St Thomas à Becket. The
dedication to the saint is one of the
earliest recorded and the row of Tudor
cottages on the approach to the church is
a delight. Walk along The Street, the
B2102, towards the eastern end of the
village. After 250m, turn left onto a
footpath through a small parking area
and alongside the recreation ground.
Cross a stile into fields, turn right and
head down across the dip and up to Sandy
Lane. Dogleg left for 75m along the lane,
then right past cottages and through a
patch of woodland into fields again.
Descend two fields and then head more
steeply down through a wood. Cross the
meadow beyond to the Tickerage Stream
and turn right onto the Wealdway.

The route now follows the stream over
two fields to a footbridge. Cross this and
fork right to follow the Wealdway to the
lane by Mill Farm. Cross the lane and
continue eastwards along the field edges,
over Pound Lane and below a house called
Tickerage Castle. The Wealdway now
heads along the edges of three fields, with
the Tickerage Stream away on the right, to
a stile onto a driveway.

Bear right along the driveway over the
stream and past the entrance to Tickerage
Mill. Continue for another 75m and fork
right off the driveway over a stile. Follow
the Wealdway uphill through woodland
and alongside fields of vines to the B2102.

◄ The landscaped grounds of Newplace

Dogleg right along the pavement for 50m, then left along a field edge down to Stonebridge Lane. Turn left down the lane for 75m and then turn right into fields. Follow the Wealdway down the left-hand edge of the large field, alongside the northern edge of Newplace Wood and over the parkland beyond towards Newplace Farm. Pass to the right of Newplace, which burned down in 1905 and was rebuilt, and follow the footpath along its driveway and round to the left down to Pump Lane.

Leave the Wealdway here and turn right up Pump Lane for 400m. Just past the cowsheds of Arches Farm bear left through a gate onto a footpath along a straight track past some ponds. Continue through a second gate and then bend right down a field edge alongside a wood. After 75m, make sure you bear right through a gate and follow the footpath down through the wood to a footbridge across a stream. Continue ahead for the final climb back up to Framfield. At the churchyard fork left and then bear right past the church and old cottages to return to the village centre.

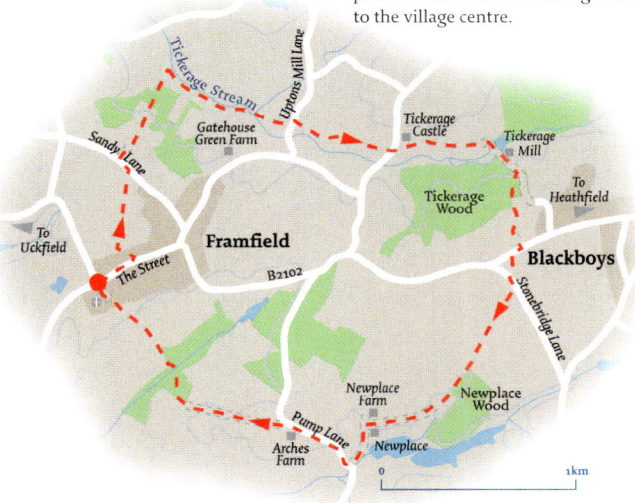

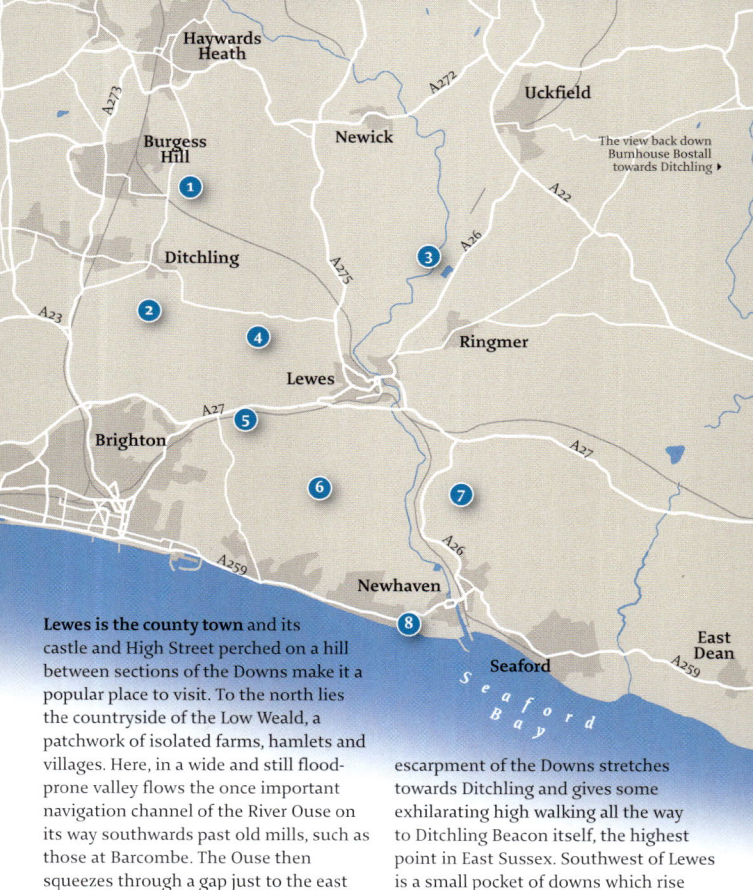

Haywards
Heath

A273

A272

Uckfield

Burgess
Hill

1

Newick

The view back down
Burnhouse Bostall
towards Ditchling ▶

A22

Ditchling

A26

3

A275

2

A23

4

Ringmer

Lewes

A27

5

A27

Brighton

6

7

A26

A259

Newhaven

8

East
Dean

Seaford

A259

Seaford Bay

Lewes is the county town and its castle and High Street perched on a hill between sections of the Downs make it a popular place to visit. To the north lies the countryside of the Low Weald, a patchwork of isolated farms, hamlets and villages. Here, in a wide and still flood-prone valley flows the once important navigation channel of the River Ouse on its way southwards past old mills, such as those at Barcombe. The Ouse then squeezes through a gap just to the east of Lewes town centre, beyond which it is channelled through estuarine marshland and past the foot of the slopes that lead to Firle Beacon to the port of Newhaven and the sea. To the west of Lewes, the escarpment of the Downs stretches towards Ditchling and gives some exhilarating high walking all the way to Ditchling Beacon itself, the highest point in East Sussex. Southwest of Lewes is a small pocket of downs which rise steeply above the village of Kingston. These slopes are far less frequented than their cousins to the north but with equally good views, especially out over the Channel.

Around Lewes

Ditchling Common Country Park

Distance 5km **Time** 1 hour 15
Terrain fields and woodland
Map OS Explorer OL11 **Access** no public
transport to the start

**Take an extended stroll over an ancient
common, well-known for its springtime
bluebells and autumn colours.**

Ditchling Common Country Park is
situated on the eastern edge of Burgess
Hill, 3km to the north of the village of
Ditchling. The walk starts from Ditchling
Common car park at the southern end of
the park on Folders Lane East, just off the
B2112. The country park is part of what
was once a much larger area of common
land. For centuries, this would have been
grazed by free-ranging cattle and sheep,
forming a mixed landscape of trees and
scrub. But after changes of land use in
the mid-20th century, the area gradually
began to return to denser woodland.
The land is once again actively managed
and much work is done by volunteers.
Parts of the common have been fenced
off for grazing and some woodland has
been coppiced. In spring, many come to
see the bluebells and wood anemones.

Take the main path out of the back of
the car park through light woodland to
the ponds. Bear right over the open
common up towards the park's top right-
hand corner. Go through the gate and take
the bridleway through the woods. After
200m, at a fork, keep right and follow the
bridleway down through woodland and

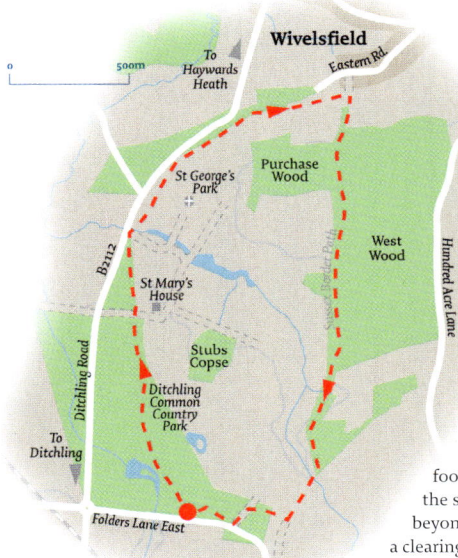

Wivelsfield

To Haywards Heath

Eastern Rd.

St George's Park

Purchase Wood

West Wood

B2112

Hundred Acre Lane

St Mary's House

Ditchling Road

Stubs Copse

Ditchling Common Country Park

To Ditchling

Folders Lane East

Border Path, which is followed for the next 2km, and head along the bridleway uphill into woodland, with West Wood on the left and Purchase Wood on the right. At the top of the rise, continue along the edge of West Wood and gently descend through the trees. This can be a very muddy section and further down there are two footbridges to help you over the small streams. About 300m beyond the footbridges you pass a clearing on the left, after which the bridleway veers a little left to a bridleway junction. At the junction, fork right with the Sussex Border Path, cross a small stream and continue up along a track past houses.

At the end of the houses by Pottery Cottage, turn right off the Sussex Border Path onto a footpath. Head past a cottage and through woodland to the entrance road to Mid Sussex Business Park. Dogleg left along the entrance road for 75m and, just before the junction with Folders Lane East, turn right onto a bridleway. Follow the bridleway for the next 150m roughly parallel with the road and over a track to the point where you can fork left back down to the car park.

along its eastern edge to emerge at the entrance road to St George's Park retirement village.

Cross the entrance road and continue along the bridleway past the retirement homes. Cross a second entrance road to St George's Park and continue along the bridleway beside the B2112 to a path junction. Leave the bridleway here and fork right onto the footpath signed for Eastern Road, over a stile and along a fenced section into fields. Follow the left-hand edge of three fields to a bridleway junction by houses on the edge of Wivelsfield.

Turn right onto the route of the Sussex

◄ The pond in Ditchling Common Country Park in early spring

Ditchling Beacon

Distance 8km **Time** 2 hours 15
Terrain fields and downland tracks
Map OS Explorer OL11 **Access** bus to
Ditchling from Lewes and Burgess Hill

Leave plenty of time to explore the village of Ditchling before climbing to the highest point on the South Downs.

The walk starts from the village of Ditchling, where parking is available in the council-owned Village Hall car park on Lewes Road. Despite the through-traffic, Ditchling remains one of the most photogenic of Sussex villages. There are many timbered buildings and the pubs and cafés are often busy. The village has a long history stretching back to Anglo-Saxon times and claims an association with Alfred the Great. St Margaret's Church is well worth a visit and contains the graves of a number of artists associated with the Arts and Crafts movement. Nearby, on Lodge Hill Lane, is the Ditchling Museum of Art and Craft, whose exhibitions chart the lives of the artists and craft workers that made the village their home during the 20th century.

From the crossroads in the village centre, walk down South Street on the route of the Sussex Border Path to the bend and junction with Beacon Road. Opposite this, take the fenced footpath signposted for The Downs between houses to reach the housing estate after 250m. Bear right into fields. The Sussex Border Path heads half-left over the first field, across the second field towards the woodland of Molehilly Shaw and along the left edge of a third field. Beyond, the route continues for 400m along a fenced path to Underhill Lane.

◄ The downs escarpment from Underhill Lane

Dogleg right along the lane for 150m, then left to continue on the Sussex Border Path along the track of Burnhouse Bostall towards the bottom of the downs escarpment. Go through a gate into Access Land and follow the path up into the coombe. The path soon bends right and steepens before veering back left and climbing up to the junction with the South Downs Way at the top of the escarpment. Go through the gate and turn left off the Sussex Border Path onto the South Downs Way. The well-waymarked trail makes its undulating way along the broad crest of the downs for the next 1.6km past two dew ponds up to the triangulation pillar at the top of Ditchling Beacon. On a clear day, you can look northwards over the Weald to the hills that include the prominent escarpment of Black Down, the highest point in Sussex.

The return route continues down to the car park beyond by Ditchling Road. Cross the road and turn left, off the South Downs Way, onto the bridleway signed for Ditchling, which descends parallel to the road for 200m before winding its way down through Ditchling Beacon Nature Reserve to Underhill Lane. Dogleg left along the lane for 75m, then right onto a bridleway down a track between houses and alongside woodland. Continue for another 300m to the left-hand bend in the track at Jointer Copse and keep ahead along the edge of the wood. Near the end of the wood, keep left at two forks and follow the byway for just under 500m down to Beacon Road. Here, a right turn along the grass verge and then the narrow pavement takes you back to the junction with South Street and the village centre.

Barcombe Mills and the River Ouse

Distance 7.5km **Time** 2 hours
Terrain riverside paths and fields (prone to flooding) and a disused railway line
Map OS Explorer OL11 **Access** very limited bus service from Lewes to Barcombe Mills Old Station (near the end of the route) or from Royal Tunbridge Wells and Uckfield to Barcombe Mills Road on the A26, 1.2km from the start

Follow a tranquil riverside route past bygone mills and an old waterside inn before returning along a disused railway line through woods and farmland.

People now flock to Barcombe Mills to enjoy the river and its setting. The mills and factory buildings producing corn, paper, linseed and even buttons beside the River Ouse have long been silent and all that remains visible are the millponds, beside which a number of information panels help explain the history of the place. The river was canalised and commercialised for the transportation of goods in the early 1800s, but was soon supplanted by the railway. Recent archaeological investigations have revealed even more of the area's history, with the discovery of a substantial Roman settlement just to the south around Bridge Farm.

Start from the Barcombe Mills car park on Barcombe Mills Road near Pikes Bridge, 5km north of Lewes off the A26. Head out the back of the car park over the Andrews Stream and then, before the bridge over the River Ouse, turn right onto the Sussex Ouse Valley Way, which is followed for the first half of the walk. The path leads through trees, across a footbridge and over the meadow beyond. It then follows the river past the embankment of Barcombe Reservoir on the right to a second footbridge. Cross over and continue beside the meandering river for the next 600m to a vehicle bridge.

◄ The River Ouse north of the Anchor Inn

The path doglegs left over the bridge, then right along the byway track for 75m to the bend by New Mill House. Keep ahead on the footpath which follows the fence around the house's garden back to the river and then bears left along the edge of the next field to the Anchor Inn.

The path crosses to the other side of the river again and continues northwards for the next 1.5km, passing under the old railway bridge and then over a series of five riverside fields to the bridleway junction by White Bridge. Turn left over the bridge and fork left through the gate, off the Sussex Ouse Valley Way, into Culpeper Nature Reserve.

The return route heads along the bridleway across the field towards the trees and over a footbridge. Bear left through woodland and, once out of the trees, continue ahead for just over 100m to a brick pillbox. Bear right here along Blunt's Lane, a grassy track which initially follows the field edge along a line of oak trees and then for the next 700m heads SSW between hedges to Anchor Lane.

Dogleg left along the lane for 200m to Anchor House and turn right onto the permissive bridleway along the line of the old railway. This path follows the disused railway's trackbed for the next 1.5km, initially through woodland and then

between fields to Barcombe Mills Road by the old station. Turn left along the road for 100m and, a little before the bus stop, fork left along the narrow lane past the entrance to Mill Farm. At the end of the lane, a right turn takes you back over the River Ouse and Pikes Bridge to the car park at the start.

Westmeston and the Downs

Distance 14km **Time** 4 hours
Terrain tracks, lanes and paths along
the tops of the downs and over fields
Map OS Explorer OL11 **Access** bus to
Westmeston from Lewes and Burgess Hill

**Long views from the top of the downs
and a series of Wealden villages make
this a delight of a walk.**

The walk starts in the village of
Westmeston, where there is some limited
parking in the small roadside lay-by
opposite St Martin's Church, which has an
unusual Norman font made of chalk
clunch in the shape of a cup. From the
junction of the B2116 with Underhill Lane
by the church, take the bridleway along
Westmeston Bostall which winds its way
for 1.2km up the escarpment of the downs
to emerge at the junction with the South
Downs Way.

Turn left and follow the well-
waymarked trail for the next 2.2km over
grassy Western Brow and then Streat Hill
before heading up the long rise over
Plumpton Plain. On a clear day there are
views northwards over the Weald and
southwards to the coast and the downs
near Brighton and Lewes. Also visible on
top of these downs are the remains of at
least four enclosed settlements dating
from the late Bronze Age, along with a
scattering of smaller domestic
settlements in the form of banked
compounds. At the entrance to the
National Trust land of Blackcap, leave the
South Downs Way, which turns right, and
keep ahead up to the triangulation pillar
on top of Blackcap.

Descend the far side for 300m to the dip
and turn left onto the bridleway down the
escarpment into the coombe. After 500m,
cross over a bridleway junction and
continue down through the next coombe
to the B2116. Cross over and follow the
bridleway over fields to Warningore Farm.

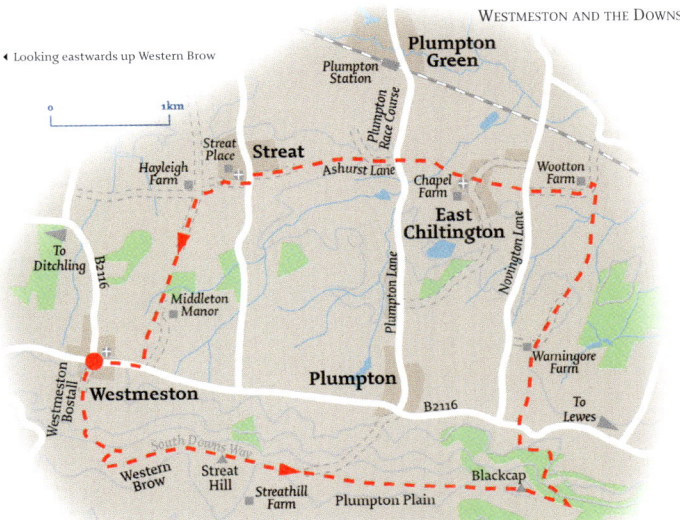

◀ Looking eastwards up Western Brow

Pass to the right of the buildings and continue along the bridleway on a clear track for 700m. At the end of a strip of woodland, where the track bends right, keep ahead on the bridleway along the right-hand edge of fields up to the buildings and houses near Wootton Farm.

Turn left past a house called The Grange and follow the footpath along the farm driveway for 500m to Novington Lane. Cross over the lane and continue westwards along the footpath over three fields to East Chiltington. Pass to the right of the church along the bridleway and head down past the entrance to Chapel Farm and across a stream. Continue up through woodland to Plumpton Lane, cross over the lane and follow the bridleway up the entrance road to Plumpton Race Course. The route

continues ahead past some houses and along a track for just under another 1km, with views left to the downs, to reach the hamlet of Streat.

Turn left along Streat Lane past the entrance to Streat Place, an Elizabethan manor house, and then fork right along the bridleway past the church. After 200m, just past Streat Cottage, fork left onto a footpath down along a field edge to the bridleway junction below the buildings of Hayleigh Farm. A left turn along the bridleway here takes you southwards for the next 1.5km between fields and then gently up through woods past Middleton Manor to the B2116. Cross the road and turn right onto the Jubilee Pathway which runs along the bank parallel with the road for 400m back to Westmeston.

Kingston and Castle Hill

Distance 8km **Time** 2 hours 30
Terrain lanes, byways and downland
paths, with a steep descent
Map OS Explorer OL11 **Access** bus to
Kingston from Lewes and Newhaven

**Follow in the footsteps of ancient drovers
and discover a long-lost hamlet in the
folds of the downs.**

The walk starts in the village of
Kingston near Lewes at the junction of
Ashcombe Lane with The Street, where
there is roadside parking along The Street.
The substantial village of Kingston, a
short distance from the town of Lewes,
lies spread out below the steep
escarpment of the downs which rise to
the west, while to the east are the fields of
the broad valley of the River Ouse.

Walk along The Street through the
oldest part of the village to St Pancras
Church, which is worth a pause to see a
rare Tapsel gate. The design supports the
weight of the gate on a central pivot and
this means that it can also be used for
resting coffins before a burial. Just past
the church, turn right along the walkway
to St Pancras Green and bear left around
the edge of the green into Church Lane.
Continue along Church Lane for 250m
past houses and then keep ahead up a
walkway to the junction with the
restricted byway of Juggs Road, an
ancient droveway which runs along the
edge of the downs between Lewes and
Brighton. A *jugg* is a Sussex term for a
basket for carrying fish, and it was along
this route that fish used to be transported
for sale in Lewes.

Turn left and follow the byway gently
uphill and through a gate. In another
150m, at a path junction, fork right to stay
on the byway. You now climb more
steeply up the north side of Castle Hill to

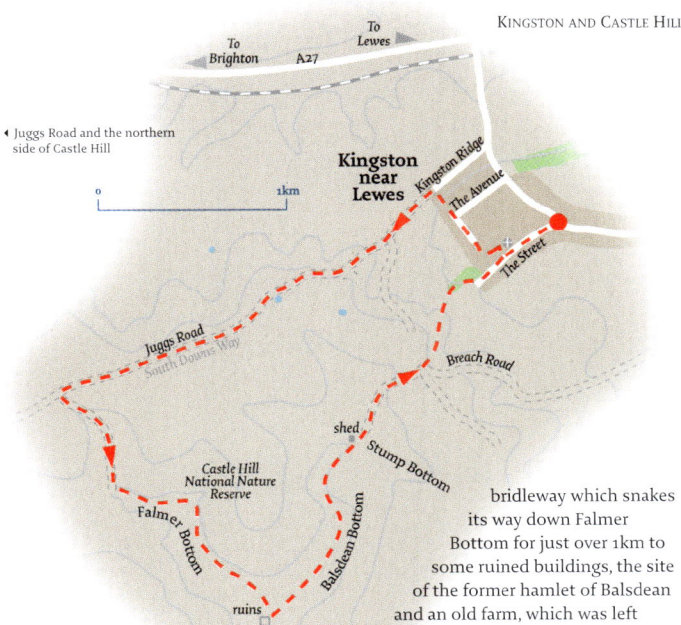

◄ Juggs Road and the northern
side of Castle Hill

**Kingston
near
Lewes**

a marker post at the junction with the
South Downs Way, which comes in from
the left. Continue ahead along the byway
over Castle Hill and down to a gate in the
dip. Just beyond the gate, the South
Downs Way turns off right but the onward
route keeps ahead for another 300m to a
bridleway crosspaths by the entrance to
Castle Hill National Nature Reserve, an
area of chalk grassland which is known
for its orchids.

Turn left down the bridleway into the
nature reserve and follow the track to the
bottom of the coombe. At the bottom,
bear left and follow the field-edge

bridleway which snakes
its way down Falmer
Bottom for just over 1km to
some ruined buildings, the site
of the former hamlet of Balsdean
and an old farm, which was left
derelict after the area was occupied by
troops during the Second World War.

By the buildings, turn left along the
bridleway which heads up Balsdean
Bottom and winds its way for the next
1km over three fields to a farm shed.
Continue ahead up the steepening track
to the bridleway junction with the South
Downs Way, which runs along the top of
the ridge. Head over the ridge and
continue down the bridleway for just 30m
before forking left onto a footpath.
Descend this steep footpath down the
north side of the hill, over two stiles and
through woodland to reach the top of The
Street in Kingston.

35

Southease, Rodmell and the River Ouse

Distance 6km **Time** 1 hour 30
Terrain lanes, riverside paths and fields
Map OS Explorer OL11 **Access** trains to
Southease Station from Brighton, Lewes,
Newhaven and Seaford (Sussex Downs
Line); bus to Rodmell village (Mill Lane
stop) from Lewes and Newhaven

**Take the train into the heart of the
Ouse Valley and follow its tidal waters
past the former home of two central
and unconventional members of the
Bloomsbury Group literary movement.**

The walk starts from Southease Station.
If arriving by car, limited roadside parking
is available halfway along the route in
Rodmell village or at the car park for the
Monk's House, if the intention is to visit.
From Southease Station, head along the
lane to the swing bridge over the River
Ouse. On the far side, turn right and pass

an information board explaining the
area's industrial past and the importance
of the River Ouse for transportation.
Follow the footpath along the raised bank
upstream alongside the tidal River Ouse,
with the Egret's Way cyclepath and
bridleway parallel on the left. There are
good views right to Itford Hill, ahead to
Mount Caburn and left to the downs
above Kingston near Lewes. The
surrounding fields are lower than the
Ouse at high tide and the bank has been
raised to prevent their flooding. It's also a
good area to spot marshland birds.

After 1.6km, just before the river bends
sharp right, take the bridleway off left
along a track between the low-lying fields.
At the gate by the water treatment works,
keep ahead to the end of the track and
follow the lane up through the village
past the Monk's House. This 16th-century

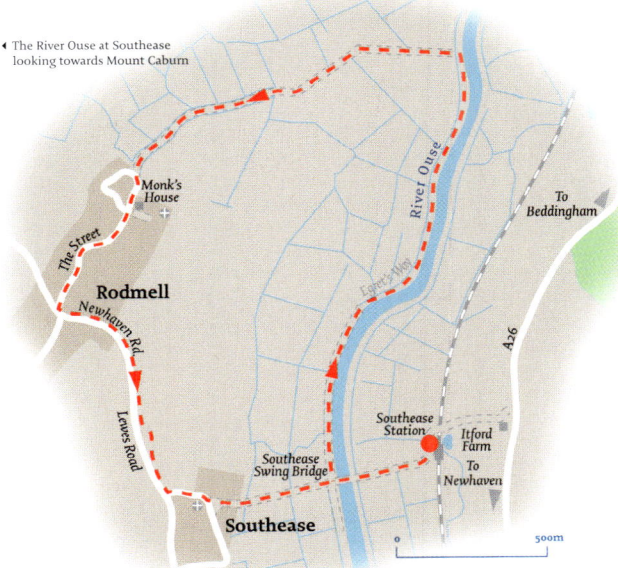

◀ The River Ouse at Southease looking towards Mount Caburn

weather-boarded house is the former home of Leonard and Virginia Woolf. They bought it as a retreat for writing away from the noise and bustle of London. The house and its cottage garden are now open to the public and include installations and exhibitions on the Bloomsbury movement and its legacy (for the restricted opening times see the National Trust's website). You can also detour left down a walkway to St Peter's Church, which has a 12th-century font with a Tudor cover and a sundial in the graveyard.

At the T-junction with Newhaven Road at the top of the village, turn left along its pavement for 200m. Where the pavement ends, continue ahead parallel to the road on a permissive path along field edges across a dip, over the rise and down into Southease village. Bear left down the lane past the church, another St Peter's. This one has a round tower, one of only three in Sussex. The other two are also in the Ouse Valley, at Piddinghoe and Lewes. Keep on down past The Green and round the left-hand bend for 400m to the swing bridge over the River Ouse again. From here, retrace your steps to the station.

Beddingham Hill and Firle Beacon

Distance 9.25km **Time** 2 hours 45
Terrain byways and downland paths
Map OS Explorer OL25 **Access** bus from
Eastbourne and Lewes to Firle (Firle Park
Gates stop, just off the A27 at the
northern edge of the village)

**Stride out from a picturesque estate
village and climb to one of the best
viewpoints on the South Downs.**

The walk starts from the village of
West Firle, also known as just Firle. There
is parking available in the village in the
visitors car park off The Street behind
The Ram Inn. Firle is an estate village
and at its heart is Firle Place, home to
the Gage family for more than 500 years
and now open to the public (see its
website for the restricted opening times).
In St Peter's Church are their family
memorials and here you'll also find
coloured stained glass by John Piper and
the graves of Duncan Grant and Vanessa

Bell, members of the Bloomsbury Group.

From the centre of Firle, head down the
track by the side of The Ram Inn, signed
for the cricket field, past the pedestrian
rear entrance to the car park. At the cricket
field, fork left past Firle Tennis Club and
head diagonally over the field beyond.
Continue through the gate, over parkland
and through the entrance gate of Firle
Place to the road junction.

Cross over and follow the footpath
which heads down the Firle Estate road
opposite, past Preston House, to a barn.
The footpath heads to the left of the barn
and along the edges of three fields across
a shallow valley to the buildings of
Preston Court Farm. Continue along the
track to the lane.

Turn left here and follow the lane up
through the hamlet of Little Dene. Beyond
the last house, the lane becomes a byway
and heads increasingly steeply up the
escarpment of Beddingham Hill. As the

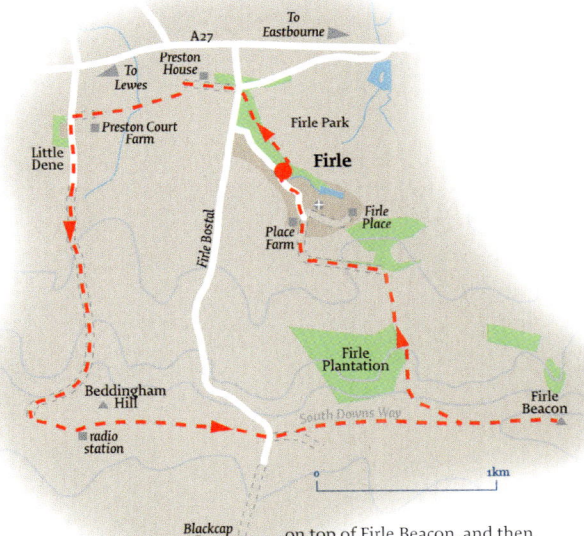

byway curves right, the gradient eases before it bends back left and climbs to the junction with the South Downs Way at the top of the escarpment.

Turn left onto the South Downs Way and follow the well-waymarked trail for the next 1.3km up past the radio transmitters on top of Beddingham Hill and along the grassy escarpment to the car park at the top of Firle Bostal. From here, it's another 1.3km of easy walking eastwards over the grassy down to a marker post below Firle Beacon. This point marks the start of the descent route back down to Firle. The route continues for a further 400m up past a Neolithic long barrow to the triangulation pillar on top of Firle Beacon, and then returns to the marker post.

On returning to the marker post, fork right off the South Downs Way and follow the bridleway which at first bears a little to the right along the edge of the escarpment for 300m and then descends more steeply around the head of a small coombe. Continue down through a gate and along a field edge to the byway running along the bottom of the escarpment.

Turn left along the field-edge byway down beside a wall and after 400m bend right to the byway junction by Place Farm. Continue ahead past the farm buildings and then along The Street past St Peter's Church and Firle Stores to return to the start in Firle.

◄ Near Little Dene looking towards Firle Beacon

Newhaven Heights

Distance 7km **Time** 2 hours
Terrain clifftop paths with sheer
drops, byway and pavements
Map OS Explorer OL11 **Access** train to
Newhaven Town Station from Lewes
and bus from Newhaven Railway Station
to Fort Road (opposite Court Farm Road
on the final section of the route)

**Combine an exhilarating and airy
clifftop walk past Newhaven Fort with a
visit to the beach.**

The walk starts from Newhaven's West
Beach near Newhaven Harbour. Parking is
available at West Beach Promenade car
park at the end of Fort Road overlooking
Newhaven Harbour, with access to the
shingle beach to its west. If visiting
Newhaven Fort, there is a dedicated car
park for visitors. Castle Hill Nature
Reserve also has a car park off Fort Road
just below the fort.

From West Beach Promenade, walk
back along Fort Road and, opposite
Newhaven Marina, turn left up Fort Rise
along the route of the England Coast
Path, which is followed to Peacehaven.
Bear right in front of Newhaven Fort and
head up through the car park. The route
now turns left up a tarmac walkway and,
after 100m, forks left to stay on the
England Coast Path.

The Coast Path heads out onto the top
of the cliffs and Castle Hill Nature
Reserve, up past the Coastguard Lookout
Station and some gun battery
emplacements. From here, you descend
past the chalets and houses of Newhaven
Heights. A gradual climb now takes you
up to the high point ahead, from where
you can see the coast stretching past
Peacehaven to Brighton and beyond. Head
down over the slight dip of Chene Gap to
the first houses of Peacehaven. You can

◄ The view from Friar's Bay Steps towards Newhaven

get down to the promenade and the beach by descending Friar's Bay Steps, which were carved into the cliff face in the 1920s. The clifftop town of Peacehaven itself was established in 1916 by the maverick entrepreneur Charles Neville. The idea was for it to be a garden city by the sea and it was laid out in a grid pattern promising health and happiness by the sea.

You now have the option of returning along the outward route, if you've not had your fill of clifftop views and the weather is fine. If it's blowing a gale, the more sheltered but less scenic route heads inland up the track towards the A259 and then turns right along The Highway, a byway, for 1.25km.

The Highway takes you up past the caravans on Rushey Hill and along a track between scrub and brambles, with intermittent views to the downs inland. You then descend past houses and the Newhaven communications mast, continuing down to the junction with Upper Valley Road. Here, turn right down a walkway and then continue ahead down Gibbon Road through the housing estate for just under 1km to Fort Road at the bottom. A right turn (passing the bus stop opposite Court Farm Road) along Fort Road, past the recreation ground and the entrance to Newhaven Fort, takes you back to West Beach.

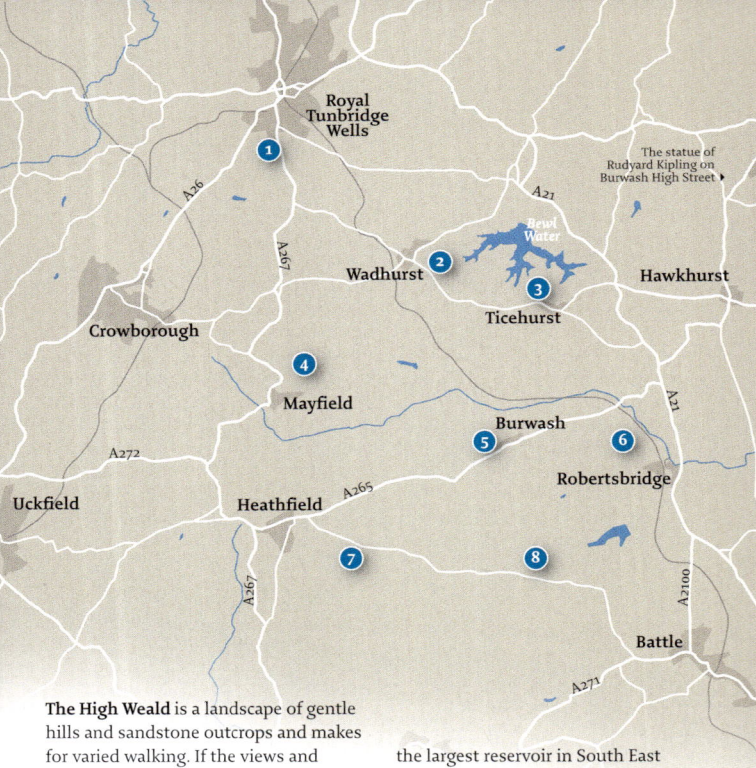

The statue of
Rudyard Kipling on
Burwash High Street ▸

The High Weald is a landscape of gentle hills and sandstone outcrops and makes for varied walking. If the views and heights are smaller in scale and route-finding a little more intricate than on the Downs, the rewards of exploring this part of East Sussex on foot can be just as satisfying. The fields tend to be small and irregularly shaped, with scattered farmsteads and villages often connected by ancient pathways. The county border with Kent and Royal Tunbridge Wells, the nearest large town, mark the northern limit of this area, with Bewl Water, now the largest reservoir in South East England and an important haven for wildlife, further to the east. The village of Frant and the A267, which leads to Heathfield, lie along the area's western edge. The River Rother is located roughly in the centre of this region and flows from west to east on its way to Rye and the English Channel. To the south among innumerable shallow valleys and patches of woodland lie the villages of Old Heathfield, Burwash, and Brightling.

Wadhurst, Heathfield and the High Weald

Frant and Eridge Park

Distance 12.5km **Time** 3 hours 30
Terrain parkland and woodland paths
Map OS Explorer 135 **Access** bus to
Frant from Royal Tunbridge Wells
and Heathfield

**If you are after peace and quiet, you'll
appreciate this longer excursion that
follows long-distance paths over a rolling
landscape of parkland, woods and fields.**

The walk starts from the pretty village
of Frant, which lies near the northern
border of the county at the edge of the
High Weald, 4km south of Royal Tunbridge
Wells. Walk past The Green, where there
is some roadside parking, and along the
A267 for 150m towards Heathfield. Turn
right with the High Weald Landscape
Trail down into woodland to a deer gate
into Eridge Old Park and cross the field
beyond into woodland.

The High Weald Landscape Trail follows
the southern edge of woodland for 500m,
bends right over a stream and crosses a
track, before continuing past a lake on the
left. It now turns left across the head of
the lake and then turns right along the
edge of woodland with Eridge Old Park on
the left. At the end of the wood, bear right
uphill alongside a fence, over the rise and
down over a track junction by the
entrance to Broadoak Fisheries into
woodland. Here, the Landscape Trail forks
right through the wood and crosses a
footbridge to a track. Cross the track and
bear right alongside a field to a stile on
the left just before a second footbridge.

At the stile, leave the Landscape Trail
and turn left along field edges to Steel
Bridge. Turn left along the lane to Steel
Bridge Farm. The route now bears right
diagonally up a field, alongside a wooded
dell and across a second field into trees.
Cross the footbridge and turn left up the
driveway to the entrance to Hamsell
Manor. The route doglegs left for 75m,

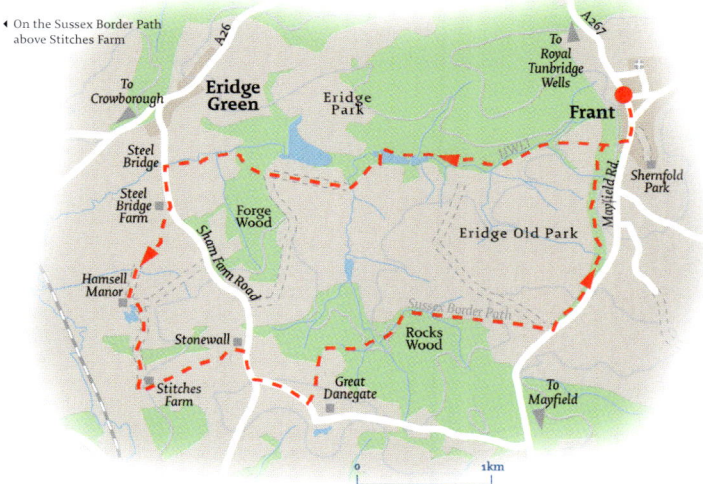

◄ On the Sussex Border Path above Stitches Farm

then right along the lane, heading steeply down across Stonewall Ghyll and uphill to Stitches Farm. Just beyond, turn left onto the Sussex Border Path. This waymarked path heads up past a barn into fields, where it doglegs left, then right along the edge of the first field. Continue uphill across two more fields and over the brow to the far side of the fourth field. The path doglegs left along the next field, then right up a sixth field to Sham Farm Road.

The Sussex Border Path now turns right up the road for 200m and then forks left along Danegate to the top of the rise. After another 100m, turn left onto a footpath which descends northwards between fields to Long Wood. Here, at a marker post, the path forks first right and then, in 100m, left downhill to a deer gate.

Beyond, head gently uphill for 500m before bending left across the stream to a marker post. A right turn here takes you eastwards along field edges and up beside Rocks Wood. Continue down across a dip, up the rough field beyond and along a line of trees to a deer gate, beyond which the path continues to the A267.

At the road, leave the Sussex Border Path and turn left up the verge for 50m to an entrance track. From here, a permissive path leads northeastwards for 450m through the strip of woodland beside the A267 and across the track to Birch Pavilion. It then bears northwards for just over 1km, down a forestry path and up to the deer gate into Eridge Old Park. From here, follow the outward route back up to Frant.

45

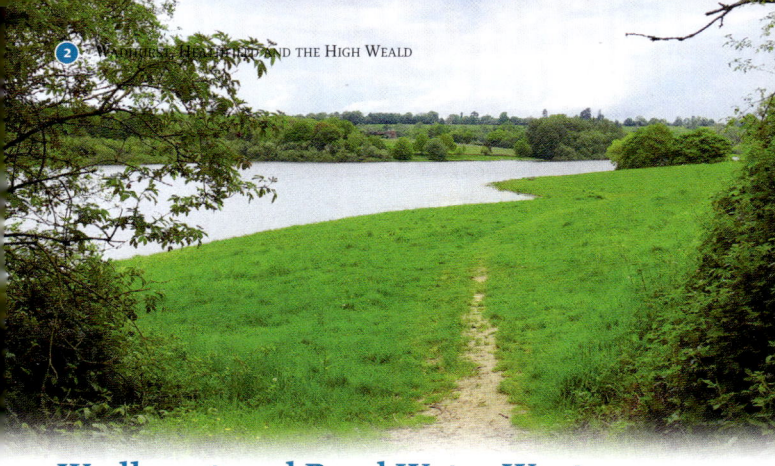

Wadhurst and Bewl Water West

Distance 7.25km **Time** 2 hours
Terrain lanes, woods and fields
Map OS Explorer 136 **Access** bus to
Wadhurst from Hawkhurst and Royal
Tunbridge Wells

**This little jewel of a stroll exploring
undulating countryside begins from one
of Sussex's most popular market towns.**

Wandering around Wadhurst, you easily
gain a sense of its history. The modern
B2099 now passes along the High Street
but this is in origin an ancient drovers'
route through the Weald and it became a
turnpike route in the 18th century. There
are many buildings which survive from
this period, and earlier, and the town still
boasts a good number of independent
shops. The name Wadhurst is a reminder
of the woods which were once crucial for
the area's iron industry and the Church of
St Peter and Paul contains a large number

of iron memorial slabs. The most recent
significant change to the area came in
the 20th century with the creation of
Bewl Water, whose western arm is passed
along the route.

From the High Street in the centre of
Wadhurst opposite Greyhound Lane and
the entrance to Greyhound car park, head
down Blacksmiths Lane for just under
400m to the bend and keep ahead to Little
Pell Farm. Pass to the left of the
farmhouse and buildings to a gate into
fields. The route now follows the footpath
along the track downhill between fields
and past a small lake. Just beyond, where
the track bends left into a field, keep
ahead with the footpath through the trees
to a stile. Continue down the left edge of
the field beyond to a junction with a
bridleway at the end of the southwestern
arm of Bewl Water.

Turn right along the bridleway which

◄ The western arm of Bewl Water

twists and turns its way for the next 1.5km around the southwestern end of the reservoir through woodland and around a small headland before circling around Browns Inlet to a prominent path junction. Here, turn right with the bridleway, signed for the Bewl Water Route, and zigzag uphill to the driveway just above Newbarn. Turn right up the driveway for 250m to the junction with Ward's Lane.

Turn right here to head up the lane for 600m, then just over the rise take the footpath off right into fields. The footpath descends the right-hand field edge before bending left down across a stream. Climb up the far side of the valley beside a wood and bend round to the right to the lane by Little Whiligh.

The route turns left steeply up the lane for 400m to Whiligh, a Grade II listed house dating from the 16th century with a grand view across the valley to Wadhurst and its church spire. Here, take the footpath off right down the field and veer left to a gate at the bottom. Once through the gate, fork left through woodland and cross over a stream into the next field. The footpath bears left and climbs steadily up the field edge and alongside a wood to the driveway to Foxhole. Cross the driveway and bear half left over the field beyond to the B2099 at the southern edge of Wadhurst. A right turn up the pavement for just over 500m takes you back to the centre of the village.

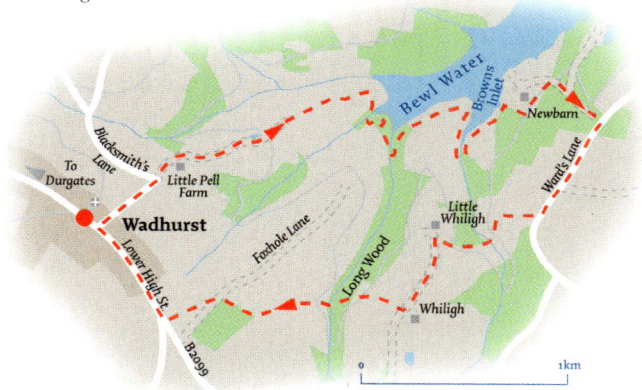

Ticehurst and Bewl Water East

Distance 7.5km (shorter option 5.5km)
Time 2 hours (shorter option 1 hour 30)
Terrain fields, woodland and paths beside
the reservoir **Map** OS Explorer 136
Access bus to Ticehurst from Hawkhurst
and Royal Tunbridge Wells

**Take a picnic and a pair of binoculars to
make the most of this route beside a
well-known reservoir.**

The walk starts from the centre of the
village of Ticehurst, where there is some
parking available, and takes you
northwards to the eastern end of Bewl
Water. This reservoir is now the largest in
South East England and for more than
50 years has been supplying drinking
water to people and towns in Kent and
Sussex. The grounds around the reservoir
are now managed in conjunction with

The Woodland Trust and Sussex Wildlife
Trust and have become increasingly
popular with walkers and cyclists.

From the junction of Church Street with
the High Street by the old well and war
memorial, walk up the High Street for
75m in the direction of Wadhurst and take
the footpath off right down a narrow
passageway to a gate into fields. Follow
the field edges in a northerly direction for
the next 1km up over the rise, down
through a patch of woodland and up the
field beyond to Tinkers Lane. Cross over
the lane and continue ahead along the
byway past Walter's Farm down to a
stream. After another 100m, turn right
down a bridleway to an inlet at the
southeastern end of Bewl Water.

Turn left for the next 1.2km along the
bridleway, which heads through

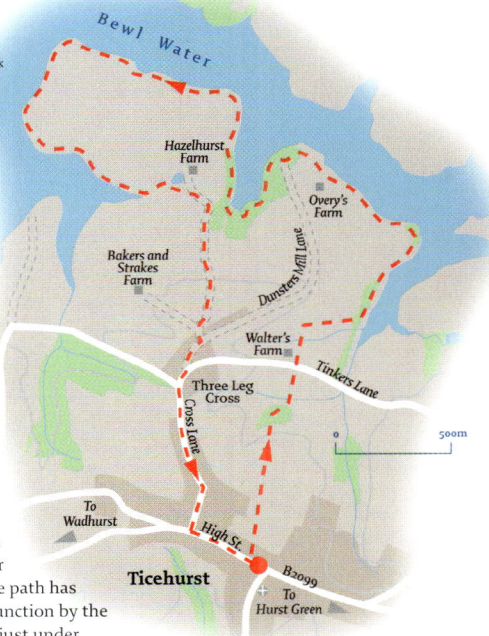

◄ Overy's Farm near Dunsters car park

woodland and then bears left alongside the shoreline past the twin oast chimneys of Overy's Farm to Dunsters car park. The bridleway doglegs right, then left here and continues for just under 500m along the shore of the inlet by Dunsters Mill House, before bending right past the head of the inlet to a path junction by gates.

At this point, the longer option continues ahead for a little over 2km along the permissive path around the next peninsula or, if you wish for a shorter option (or if the permissive path has been closed), at the path junction by the gates you can turn left for just under 100m up to the track which then leads off left to Three Leg Cross.

The longer option heads northwards and circles left around the western shoreline of the peninsula to a junction with a bridleway by a footbridge at Grebe Corner at the head of the small inlet on its southern side. Turn left onto the bridleway here, head up some steps and bear to the right past a house to the junction with the track which leads to Three Leg Cross, and turn right.

The track, which carries a footpath, gently rises between fields for 600m to Dunsters Mill Lane at the edge of the hamlet of Three Leg Cross. Turn right along the road through the hamlet to the junction. Here, fork left onto Cross Lane which winds its way for just under 700m gently uphill over the rise to the B2099 at the western edge of Ticehurst. Turn left down the pavement for 300m to return to the centre of the village.

49

Mayfield and Sharnden

Distance 8km **Time** 2 hours 15
Terrain lanes and tracks through
woodland and field paths
Map OS Explorer 136 **Access** bus to
Mayfield from Heathfield and
Royal Tunbridge Wells

**This varied walk with some fine
views begins from a quintessential
Sussex village.**

Mayfield had close links to the iron
industry and has a 16th-century cannon
on display on its High Street. The Saxon
St Dunstan, to whom the church is
dedicated, was not only Archbishop of
Canterbury, but also a skilled smith.
While St Dunstan was busy in his forge,
the devil, disguised as a beautiful woman,
came to tempt him. St Dunstan was not
fooled and used his hot tongs to despatch
him. The nearby village sign carries an
unusual skulking red devil to this day.

From the High Street in Mayfield near
St Dunstan's Church and the village sign,
cross the road, head down narrow Holders
Lane, signed for the car park on South
Street, and turn left down The Avenue to
the junction with Fletching Street. Turn
right down the hill for 250m and, by a
small green, fork right onto East Street,
signed for Broad Oak and Witherenden.
Follow the pavement past houses and
then keep along the lane for another 700m
to the right bend.

Here, the route forks left onto the
bridleway down the tree-lined track to
Merrieweathers Farm. After 300m, the
bridleway forks left off the track down a
sunken way and then past Merrieweathers
House to a bridleway track junction. The
route turns left onto the track, which
crosses a bridge over a stream and then
winds its way up over the rise and down
to a path junction at a left bend near the

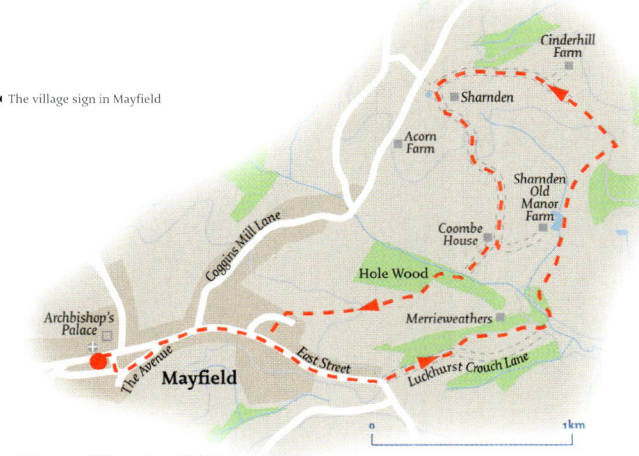

◀ The village sign in Mayfield

buildings of Sharnden Old Manor Farm.

At the bend, leave the track and keep ahead onto the footpath which leads through a gate and climbs gently up the valley along the edge of two fields to a footpath junction in the strip of woodland at the top. Turn left and follow the footpath along the top edge of the woodland to a gate by Cinderhill Cottage. The route continues past the cottage and along the lane for 800m, past the turn for Cinderhill Farm and up round the left bend, to a bridleway junction by the entrance to Sharnden.

Turn left onto the bridleway through the entrance and then bear right down an unusual track of concrete railway sleepers, signed for Sharnden Old Manor. The sleepers were originally on the bed of the railway line that ran through Heathfield and were brought here by the lorryload after the line closed. The track winds its way downhill between fields for the next 1km past the entrance to Sharnden Old Manor and then more steeply down to a footpath junction by Coombe House.

A short dogleg right below the house, then left over a stile takes you down the right edge of a field to the valley bottom and into Hole Wood. The footpath crosses a footbridge and bears right alongside the stream for 75m before turning left uphill to the top of the wood. Continue out of the trees and fork left along the field edge up a line of trees to a crosspaths at the top. Cross over a sunken way and keep ahead over the next field. The route then passes along the backs of houses to Southmead Close. Cross over and continue on the footpath along the narrow passageway to East Street, where a right turn will take you back up Fletching Street to the centre of Mayfield.

Burwash

Distance 9km **Time** 2 hours 30
Terrain fields, lanes and woodland over
undulating countryside
Map OS Explorer 136 **Access** bus to
Burwash from Uckfield and Hurst Green

**Amble over rolling countryside with
some pleasant views and the chance to
visit a well-known Jacobean mansion.**

Many people come to Burwash to visit
Bateman's, the former home of the author
and Nobel Laureate Rudyard Kipling. The
house, now managed by the National
Trust, is passed along the route but it is
also worth venturing along the High
Street where you can see a modern statue
of the author by local sculptor Victoria
Atkinson, and, further on near St
Bartholomew's Church, the village war
memorial, on which is inscribed among
those who died in the First World War the
name of his son, John.

From the High Street in Burwash, take
the footpath past the Bear Inn and council
car park into fields. Head down the right
edge of the first field for 100m, bear right
into the next one and then follow the
waymarks across this field and down
three more to Bateman's Lane. Turn right
along the lane for 200m to Bateman's,
where you can find the visitors' entrance
to the house and gardens up to the right.

The route turns left onto a bridleway
along the lane over the River Dudwell and
continues for 200m round the right bend
to some cottages. By Corner Cottage, turn
right onto a footpath past the old
watermill and circle anticlockwise around
the millpond. On the far side, the path
continues between fields and round the
left bend to a path junction.

Turn right to cross the footbridge back
over the River Dudwell into fields. The
route crosses the first field and then turns
left along the bottom edge of the second
onto a wooded path that leads past a

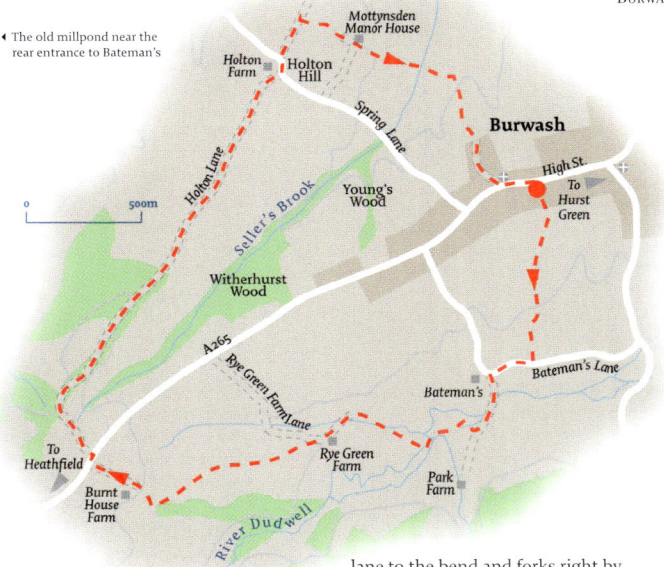

◀ The old millpond near the
rear entrance to Bateman's

small ruined building and up a track to a
lane by the cottages of Rye Green Farm.
Cross the lane and, for the next 700m,
head up a series of four fields, before
turning right up a fifth field to the houses
and buildings of Burnt House Farm. From
here, continue up the driveway for 250m
to Weald House by the A265.

Cross the road with care and dogleg
right for 30m along the verge, then left
onto the bridleway along Holton Lane
which heads up past houses and then
bends left downhill. After 150m, bear right
and walk northeastwards for just under
2km along the undulating and tree-lined
bridleway to Spring Lane at Holton Hill.

The route turns left for 75m along the

lane to the bend and forks right by
Franchise Lodge onto the bridleway which
heads down the driveway for 250m past an
airman's memorial to a crosspaths. Turn
right and follow the waymarks downhill
along the edges of two fields to
Mottynsden House and then continue
down its driveway to Mottynsden Manor.
Keep ahead down the next field and cross
the footbridge at the valley bottom. The
footpath now heads up the fields on the
far side for 150m and turns right over a
second footbridge onto a fenced path,
which rises gently between fields to
Dawes Farm. Bear right steeply up the
driveway past houses to the western end
of the High Street in Burwash and turn
left to return to the centre of the village.

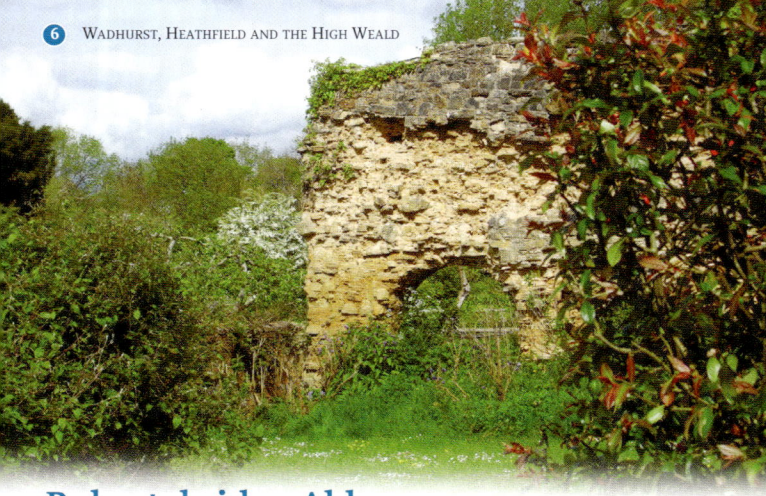

Robertsbridge Abbey

Distance 6km **Time** 1 hour 45
Terrain lanes, bridleways and woodland
paths **Map** OS Explorer 124 **Access** bus to
Robertsbridge from Hawkhurst and
Hastings; train to Robertsbridge from
Hastings and Royal Tunbridge Wells

**Follow in the footsteps of medieval
monks on this simple stroll past a long-
vanished abbey.**

The walk starts from the village of
Robertsbridge, where parking is available
at the car park on Station Road. Today
Robertsbridge is a pretty enough Wealden
village, still dominated by tile-hung
weather-boarded and timber-framed
buildings. The nearby A21 carries most of
the through-traffic but has had the
disadvantage of somewhat cutting off the
village from the land to the east, where

you'll find the remains of its medieval
Cistercian abbey.

From the High Street, head up Fair Lane
past old cottages to the top and fork right
onto the pedestrian bridge over the A21.
Bear left down to Fair Lane and continue
along it to the farm buildings at Redlands.
Keep ahead onto the bridleway along the
private road between fields for the next
1km to the modern houses by the ruins of
Robertsbridge Abbey, visible on the left
through the gate to The Abbey, formerly a
farmhouse but now a private residence.

This was originally the Abbot's House
and is the main surviving part of the
abbey, which functioned until the
dissolution of the monasteries in the 16th
century. In the garden are all that remains
in situ of the rest of the abbey. In later
years, many of its stones and timbers

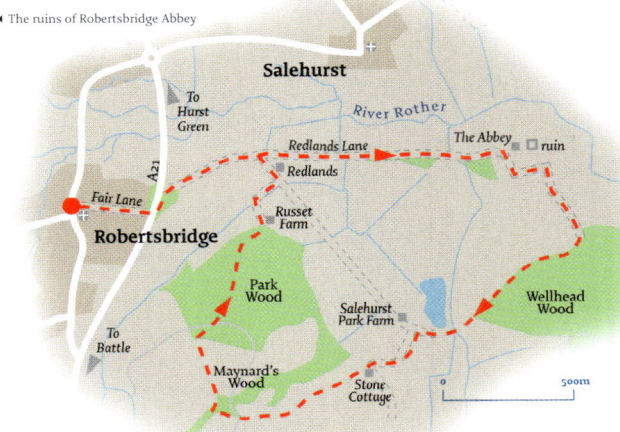

◄ The ruins of Robertsbridge Abbey

were used in the construction of houses in the village.

Continue through the bends to a gate and path junction. In front of the gate, turn right and follow the bridleway around a modern house and its garden and then bear right along a track to the bridleway junction by Wellhead Wood. Fork right along a track and then almost immediately bear right to stay on the bridleway, which rises gently up the northern edge of the wood, over a rise and down to a bridleway junction at its western edge. Keep ahead along the field edge beyond to a gate onto a track by a small house.

Head along the track to a junction and turn left uphill for 250m to the crosspaths by Stone Cottage. Keep ahead on the bridleway through the trees and up along the edge of a field. For the next 500m, the bridleway winds its way gently uphill and bends right into the top of Maynard's Wood to a path junction.

Turn right and follow the footpath along the top edge of Maynard's Wood and over a field to the corner of Park Wood. Follow the footpath down into the wood. After 50m, at a footpath junction, keep ahead downhill and ignore other paths off left and right. Near the bottom of the wood, pass over a crosspaths and descend to a stile by the buildings of Russet Farm. Bear left down the field to a driveway. Turn right down the driveway and then left to reach the buildings at Redlands once again. From here, turn left and retrace your steps along Fair Lane, over the A21 and back down into Robertsbridge.

Old Heathfield and St Dunstan's Wood

Distance 4.25km **Time** 1 hour 15
Terrain fields and woodland, some parts
can be muddy **Map** OS Explorer OL25
Access no public transport to the start

**Enjoy a short and secluded stroll on the
edge of the bustling town of Heathfield.**

The walk starts from the village of Old
Heathfield, where there is roadside
parking on School Hill opposite the
cricket ground, just up from All Saints'
Church. The village of Old Heathfield is
the original settlement of Heathfield, now
the far larger neighbouring market town,
separated from it by Heathfield Park. The
church has an unusual 20th-century
stained glass window commemorating
one of its vicars, Robert Hunt, and the
establishment of the first permanent
English settlement in North America at
Jamestown, Virginia, in 1607. Hunt had

arrived in Heathfield from Kent five years
previously but was obliged by his
parishioners to leave after talk of
immorality. He made arrangements to sail
for the New World and after a four-month
journey made landfall at the mouth of
Chesapeake Bay. The story is that Hunt
delivered his first sermon under the
sailcloth of the very ship he had sailed in.
The Jamestown settlement was plagued
by difficulties and within a year Hunt had
died of illness and was buried in the
church he helped to found.

Walk down School Hill to the church, go
through the lychgate and fork left down
through the extensive graveyard to a gate
into fields. Keep on down the field beyond
to a footbridge and climb up the field on
the far side to a stile onto a track. The
route heads up the track for 250m and
then turns right along the field edge to

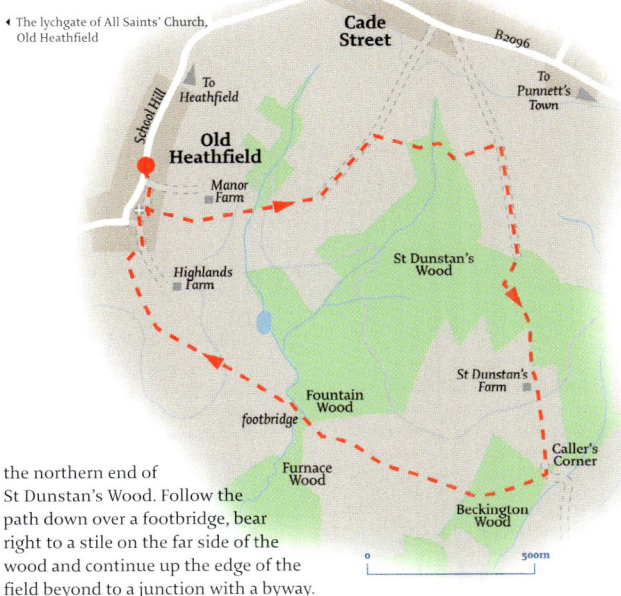

◄ The lychgate of All Saints' Church, Old Heathfield

Cade Street

B2096

To Heathfield

To Punnett's Town

School Hill

Old Heathfield

Manor Farm

Highlands Farm

St Dunstan's Wood

St Dunstan's Farm

Fountain Wood

footbridge

Furnace Wood

Caller's Corner

Beckington Wood

0   500m

the northern end of St Dunstan's Wood. Follow the path down over a footbridge, bear right to a stile on the far side of the wood and continue up the edge of the field beyond to a junction with a byway.

Turn right onto the narrow byway and descend gently to a gate that leads back into St Dunstan's Wood. Follow the track ahead for 100m, then fork left to continue in a southerly direction down to a gate into fields. The route now heads down the edges of three fields to the path junction by Caller's Corner and the entrance track to St Dunstan's Farm.

Turn right over the track onto the footpath up through Beckington Wood to a stile into fields. The route now heads over the middle of the first field, follows the waymarks across the rough second field over the brow and continues down a

track, with Fountain Wood off to the right. At the bottom bear right with the track over a stream and up round the left bend.

Here, the footpath forks right off the track into fields again. Head up the left edge of the first field, cross over a track and follow the right edge of two more fields down to a gate. Climb up the third field with the houses of Old Heathfield visible ahead and bear right through a gate. Cross over the driveway of Heathfield House and then the grass area beyond to Church Street, where a left turn up past the entrance to the Star Inn brings you back to the church.

57

Brightling Follies

Distance 6.75km (including detour)
Time 2 hours **Terrain** fields, lanes and
woodland **Map** OS Explorer 124
Access no public transport to the start

**A country stroll with a difference takes
you through fields and parkland on a
tour of some unusual follies.**

The walk starts from the small village of
Brightling, where there is some limited
parking on the roadside in the village and
in a small lay-by opposite the village hall.
The walk passes a series of unusual
structures, built by John 'Mad Jack' Fuller,
a wealthy 18th-century industrialist and
politician, who lived at Brightling Park
and whose substantial wealth came, in
part, from slave estates in Jamaica.

The first of the follies is the unmissable
stone pyramid in the churchyard,
reminiscent of a Roman or Egyptian
mausoleum and under which Fuller was
ostentatiously buried. On the route, you

encounter The Tower, whose Gothic style
is reminiscent of Bodiam Castle, which
Fuller also restored; The Temple is a
domed neoclassical rotunda, rumoured to
have been used as a gambling den; next is
the 10m-high cone called The Sugar Loaf
marking the southern edge of the park;
the final two monuments are The
Observatory, designed by Robert Smirke,
of British Museum fame, and now a
private house, and The Obelisk, thought
to have been built to commemorate
Wellington's victory over Napoleon.

From the southeast side of the
churchyard by the entrance to Brightling
Park, walk down the lane to the junction
and take the footpath opposite into fields.
The route heads over two fields, along a
fenced section in the third field and turns
right up the field edge to The Tower,
which is surrounded by trees. Continue
down the field beyond to the lane, with a
view ahead to The Temple.

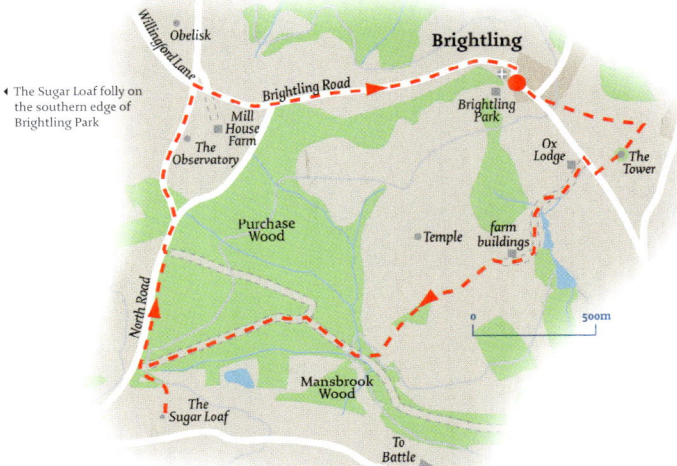

◄ The Sugar Loaf folly on
the southern edge of
Brightling Park

Dogleg right along the lane for 75m, then left through the entrance to Ox Lodge onto a bridleway. Head down the track and bend left past a lake and the cricket ground to a path junction. The route now turns right onto a footpath, signed for The Sugar Loaf, which heads up past some farm buildings and turns left along the edges of two fields to some woodland, with a view right up to The Temple. Continue through the trees, down across a field and into Mansbrook Wood to a footbridge over a stream.

Turn right here onto a bridleway that follows a forestry track for 250m to a track junction. Turn left off the bridleway up a pleasant path through the mixed woodland of Purchase Wood to a path junction just before the lane at the wood's southwestern corner. From here, you can detour out and back to The Sugar Loaf by

continuing ahead to the lane, then turning sharp left onto a footpath up past a works yard and over a field (350m round trip).

The onward route from the path junction at the corner of Purchase Wood turns right and follows the path northwards alongside a wall at the edge of the wood up to a small parking area. Join the lane here and in 150m fork left, signed for Burwash, to climb steeply up Observatory Road to The Observatory at the top of the rise.

Continue down the lane, from which there is a good view of The Obelisk. At the junction turn right, signed for Brightling, along Sheepshaw Lane to the next junction and then keep ahead along Long Reach for the final 1km past Avenue Lodge, across the dip and up round the bend into Brightling.

If Eastbourne as a seaside town has a reputation for being rather staid and unexciting, the same cannot be said for the walking it has on offer. To the west of the town lie Beachy Head and the Seven Sisters, which provide some of the most dramatic walking along the entire length of the South Downs. For this reason alone, many walking the South Downs Way choose to finish here rather than at the route's western end. Here too, in a gap in the downs, you will find the much-frequented village of Alfriston and the River Cuckmere, whose final meanderings

before reaching Cuckmere Haven have become one of the defining images of this part of the county, if not of the entire south coast of England. In stark contrast, to the east lies the expanse of Pevensey Levels, an area of marsh reclaimed from the sea and criss-crossed by reed-fringed ditches and small lanes, whose southern limits are still guarded by its famous Norman castle. If gentler walking is required then the area inland from Eastbourne provides a number of options in the countryside surrounding the villages of Chiddingly, Hellingly, Herstmonceux and Arlington.

Around Eastbourne

Chiddingly and Gun Hill

Distance 6.5km **Time** 1 hour 45
Terrain paths, lanes and tracks over
fields and through woods
Map OS Explorer OL25 **Access** no public
transport to the start

**Combine a classic country walk with the
chance to visit an historic church, a
sculpture garden, two village pubs and a
nearby former artists' home.**

The walk starts from the village of
Chiddingly, where the tall stone spire of
its church is a prominent landmark.
Inside the church is the enormous Jefferay
Monument, one of only two of its type in
England. The monumental alabaster
sculpture commemorates the Jefferay
family, lords of the manor in the 15th and
16th centuries. The village also has a
connection with more modern forms of
art. The 20th-century surrealist artist
Roland Penrose and photographer Lee
Miller lived at nearby Farleys House,
whose galleries and gardens are now open
to the public. Pablo Picasso stayed with
the couple and visited the village on his
visit to England in 1950 to address the
World Peace Conference in Sheffield. Next
to the car park in the village centre, you
will find the Millennium Oak Sculpture
and Garden, where Picasso's 'Dove of
Peace' is celebrated. The sculptures were
created by the artist Anthony Padgett and
unveiled in 2022 as part of the Picasso
Peace Project.

From the centre of Chiddingly by The
Six Bells pub, walk along Church Lane
past the large free car park to the church.
Go round the left bend past the entrance
to the church and then bear left with the
Wealdway path through a gate into fields.
At the path junction immediately beyond
the gate, take the left fork, following the
Wealdway over two fields down to a
footbridge over a stream in woodland.
Climb up the field beyond to a lane.

◀ The Six Bells pub in Chiddingly

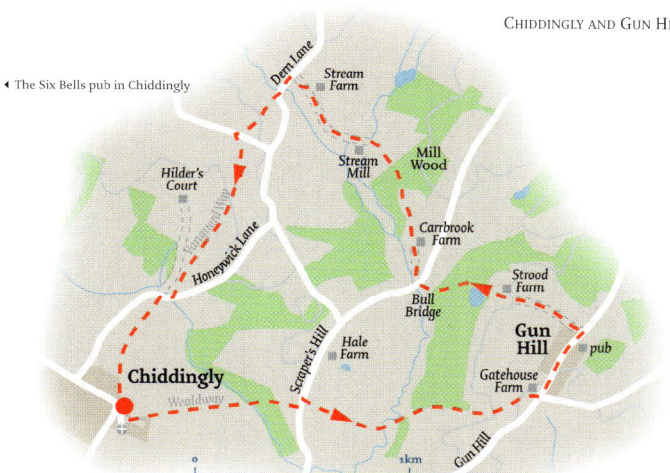

Dogleg briefly left up the lane, then right to stay on the Wealdway, which continues along the track past Hale Farm Campsite down to a footbridge. Cross this and bear left through the small wood. The footpath continues along the left-hand edge of the long field beyond and over the rise in the next field to the lane by Gatehouse Farm.

Turn left along the lane for 400m past the houses of Gun Hill and, just beyond The Gun pub, take the bridleway off left along the track to Strood Farm. At the farm, keep on through the buildings to a gate, beyond which the bridleway continues down alongside woodland to the lane by Bull Bridge.

Cross over the lane and follow the footpath along the track through the buildings of Carrbrook Farm to Mill Wood. Take the footpath which forks left through the wood and, at the far side,

descend the left-hand edge of a field to a bridleway junction by Stream Mill. Bear left along the bridleway, cross over a large footbridge and continue for 300m to a driveway by Stream Farm, which in the 16th century was the site of an ironworks. Turn left down the driveway to Dern Lane.

Head left down the lane to the bend and, just over the stream, take the footpath off right up beside a field to Stalkers Lane. Cross over the lane and follow the Vanguard Way along the double-fenced path between fields, with the spire of Chiddingly Church visible ahead, for just under 1km down to Honeywick Lane. A short dogleg right along the lane, then left keeps you on the Vanguard Way, which heads uphill along the edges of fields and over the rise to bring you back to Church Lane in Chiddingly.

Hellingly and the Cuckoo Trail

Distance 3km **Time** 45 minutes
Terrain former railway track, field paths
and lanes **Map** OS Explorer OL25
Access bus to Hellingly from Hailsham,
Heathfield and Eastbourne

**Take a short stroll from a small attractive
village along a former railway line that's
popular with walkers and cyclists.**

This short walk starts from the Cuckoo
Trail car park on Station Road at the
eastern edge of Hellingly village, which
lies just to the north of the town of
Hailsham. The Cuckoo Trail is a shared
route for walkers, cyclists and horse riders
which follows a section of the former
railway line that ran between Polegate,
Heathfield and Eridge until the 1960s. The
name of the line originated among the
workers who constructed the railway and
who attended the annual 'Heffle' Fair at
Heathfield, where the first cuckoo of
spring was traditionally heard.

Walk out the rear of the small car park
past the old railway station and turn
left onto the Cuckoo Trail along the
disused railway line. Follow the trail in
the direction of Horam and Heathfield
between houses and through woodland
with the Cuckmere River on the left.
Cross Mill Lane and continue to the
footbridge over the river. In another
400m, you come to Shawpits Bridge,
which has some wildlife sculpture panels
on its walls.

Pass under the bridge and turn left off
the Cuckoo Trail onto a footpath. Go
through two gates and along a permissive
path on the left-hand edge of the field.
After 50m, bear left through a gate and
continue on the other side of the hedge to
the corner of the field. Bear left and follow
the right-hand edge to the end of the
field. Go through a gate and cross a
footbridge over a stream. Keep along the
edge of the third field for 50m and then

◄ Approaching Shawpits Bridge on the Cuckoo Trail

turn right through a large gate. Follow the edge of the fourth field to the far end, where you should bear a little to the right to a high stile down to a sunken path. Turn left for just over 100m to reach Church Lane.

Bear left up Church Lane and over the rise to the junction with Vicarage Lane. Fork right past Corner Cottage and continue down Church Lane, which descends gently for 400m past houses to St Peter and St Paul Church in Hellingly. Bear left through the oval churchyard, a mark of its Saxon origins, past a delightful row of old tile-hung cottages on the left to a gate on the far side onto Mill Lane by the junction with Station Road. Turn left along Station Road for 350m to return to the Cuckoo Trail car park.

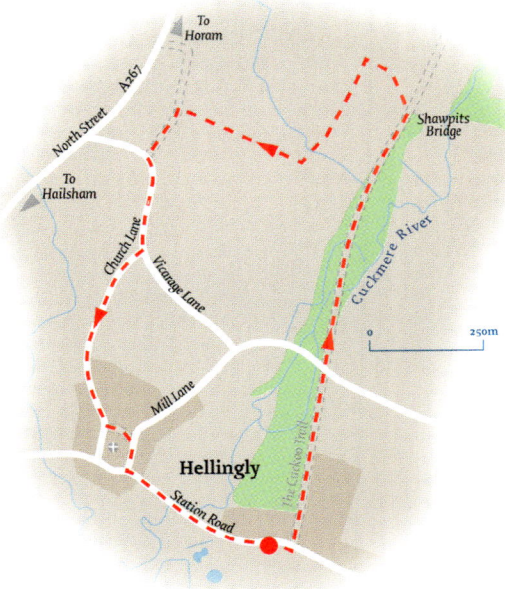

Herstmonceux and Pevensey Levels

Distance 10.5km **Time** 3 hours
Terrain fields, lanes, marsh and parkland
Map OS Explorer 124 **Access** bus to
Herstmonceux from Eastbourne
and Hastings

Make a day of it and combine this varied route with a visit to a striking 15th-century red-brick moated castle.

The walk starts from the village of Herstmonceux and passes the entrance to Herstmonceux Castle and its extensive grounds and gardens, which are open to the public. Most visitors arrive by car but Herstmonceux Castle Estate welcomes visitors who arrive on foot.

In Herstmonceux at the junction of Hailsham Road and Gardner Street by the school, take the footway past the recreation ground into fields. Bear half-right across the first field and then walk down three more fields over Lime Park to reach a gate. At the track beyond, dogleg right, then left and continue over two

more fields down to a footbridge. Climb the field beyond to Butler's Lane. Turn right down the lane for 600m to the junction, with a view ahead to Wilmington Hill. Turn left along Lower Road for 100m and take the footpath off right onto Pevensey Levels.

Head over the first field, cross the footbridge over the stream and turn right, parallel with the stream, to a hedge. Bear left along it and after 150m fork left to a gateway over a ditch. From here, the route follows the right of way southwards for 500m over two ditches to a footbridge. Continue to the next footbridge and across the field beyond to a path junction at another ditch near the road.

Turn left onto the footpath which heads alongside the ditch and then the wider channel of Hurst Haven for 400m. At the second gate, the footpath leaves Hurst Haven and bears half-left over the marsh to a gateway over a ditch. Here, take the path off right over the marshy field to a

Herstmonceux

Gardner St.

◄ Looking across the northern
part of Pevensey Levels

Lime
Park

A271

To
Hailsham

Chapel Row

**Windmill
Hill**

To
Boreham
Street

Butler's
Farm

Butler's Lane

Flowers
Green

Place
Farm

Lower Road

Herstmonceux
Place

Sackville
Farm

Wartling Road

New Bridge Road

Mill Stream

Herstmonceux
Castle

Science
Centre

Wartling
Wood

1066 Country Walk

Church
Farm

0   1km

gate onto a bridleway. Turn left and follow the 1066 Country Walk waymarks along the bridleway between fields up to All Saints Church. Inside you'll find the remarkable Dacre Memorial, a richly-coloured tomb in Gothic style.

By the church, turn right with the 1066 Country Walk and follow the bridleway downhill past the buildings of Bader College, along the edge of woodland and over a field with a view to Herstmonceux Castle. Continue up the far side of the valley to Wartling Road. Turn left past the entrance to Herstmonceux Castle and, after 50m, take the footpath off left. Head half-right up past the green domes of The Observatory Science Centre to the top of the field and follow the right of way alongside the fence down through the

woodland to a bridleway. Bear left between two small lakes and continue up a wide track for 300m to a path junction in fields just beyond a gate.

Take the bridleway off left over the field to a gate, then turn right along a hedge to a crosspaths at the top of the rise. Turn left down the field, cross a track and bear half-right up the field beyond to a small gate to the right of Place Farm. Bear left up the field edge to Church Road. Turn right for 700m up Church Road through Flowers Green to Chapel Row. Just before Herstmonceux Free Church, fork left onto a footpath down a passageway into fields. Take the path up the middle of the field, over the rise and back down past the recreation ground to return to the start.

Arlington Reservoir

Distance 5.5km **Time** 1 hour 30
Terrain reservoir path, fields and
woodland **Map** OS Explorer OL25
Access no public transport to the start

**Step back into the past on this short walk
from a picturesque reservoir to a village
with a long history.**

The walk starts from Arlington
Reservoir's car park, which has a kiosk
café and toilets. Its entrance is 1km north
of Berwick Station along Station Road.
There is also a lay-by alongside Station
Road opposite the entrance where parking
is possible. The reservoir was built by
cutting off a meander of the Cuckmere
River, across which is the village of
Arlington. Designated a Local Nature
Reserve, the area is a haven for wildlife
and gives views over the South Downs to
the Long Man of Wilmington.

Head out of the rear of the car park and
turn left onto the reservoir's circular walk.
The route heads round the northern side

of the reservoir and then rises gently away
from the water's edge up through
woodland and along its top edge to a path
junction at the top of the rise. Fork left
down the bridleway here to the far side of
the wood and a gate onto fields. Descend
the left-hand field edge and at the bottom
follow it round to the right, past the
buildings of Sessingham Farm and over a
footbridge to a junction with a byway.

Turn right along the byway for 150m to
the footbridge over the Cuckmere River,
where the Wealdway path comes in from
the left. Cross the bridge on the route of
the Wealdway and after 50m turn right
into fields. Head up the first field to some
ruined brick barns and then follow the
left-hand edge of the second field towards
the spire of Arlington Church. At the end
of the field near a large double fronted
brick barn, bear left across the corner of a
third field to reach the graveyard of St
Pancras Church.

The dedication to St Pancras, a Roman

◀ The view across Arlington Reservoir to Wilmington Hill

martyr, is often a sign that a church can be dated to the earliest period of Christianity in England. The place may have been used by Romano-British worshippers and there is evidence of Roman occupation – Roman tiles can be seen in various parts of the church and the fields between the church and the reservoir have remained unploughed in order to preserve what may well be the remains of a settlement dating back to late Roman times.

Go through the millennium lychgate (you can detour left to the village centre and the Yew Tree Inn) and turn right to a stile into fields. Cross the first field, turn right along the edge of the second and

bear left over the third to a metal footbridge across the Cuckmere River. Bear a little to the right over the field beyond and head up to the stile at the top.

Turn left and follow the footpath along the reservoir wall to the gate on its southern side. Turn right along the lane beyond to the entrance to Lakeside Farm and Polhills Farm, where the path heads to the left around the perimeter of both farms to their northern entrance. Cross the entrance track and bear left for 400m along the reservoir's circular walk back to the car park.

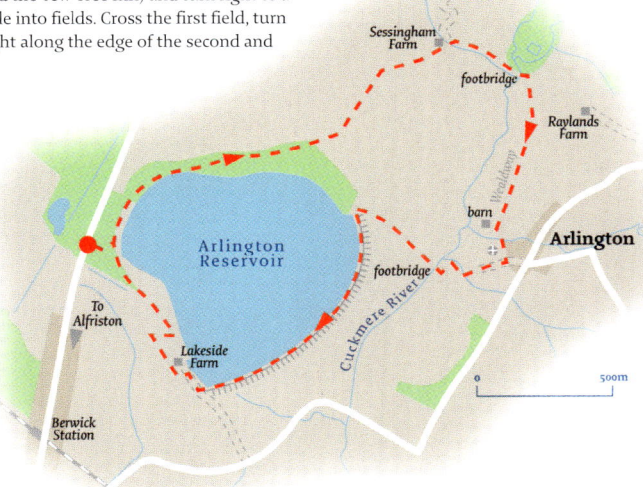

Pevensey Levels and Castle

Distance 7km **Time** 1 hour 45
Terrain fields and marshland (prone to
flooding), with a major road crossing
Map OS Explorer 124 **Access** bus to
Pevensey Castle from Eastbourne

**This walk is brimming with wildlife
and history from Roman times right up
to the present.**

The walk starts from the entrance to
Pevensey Castle at the top of the High
Street in Pevensey, where parking is
available in the Cattle Market car park.
The Norman castle has become one of
the iconic images of Sussex and is much
visited. The Romans had previously
established a fort here, called Anderida,
which was part of what has become
known as the Saxon Shore forts along the
south and east coasts. Pevensey,
however, remains most famous for
being the place where William, Duke of
Normandy, landed with his fleet before
engaging and defeating King Harold at
the Battle of Hastings. The castle is open
to the public and is managed by English
Heritage. Entry to the outer curtain of the
castle grounds is free. Nearby St Nicolas
Church is also well worth a visit and
contains a series of panels outlining
Pevensey's history.

From the castle entrance, follow the
route of the 1066 Country Walk down
Castle Road and, before the end of the
castle wall, turn right down a track to the
A27. The road is often busy but the
section is straight and visibility is good
for crossing. Continue along a fenced
footpath and bend left along Martin's
Ditch to a gate. The route continues to
follow the 1066 Country Walk for the next
3km over the fields beside Pevensey
Haven. You pass a footbridge, which

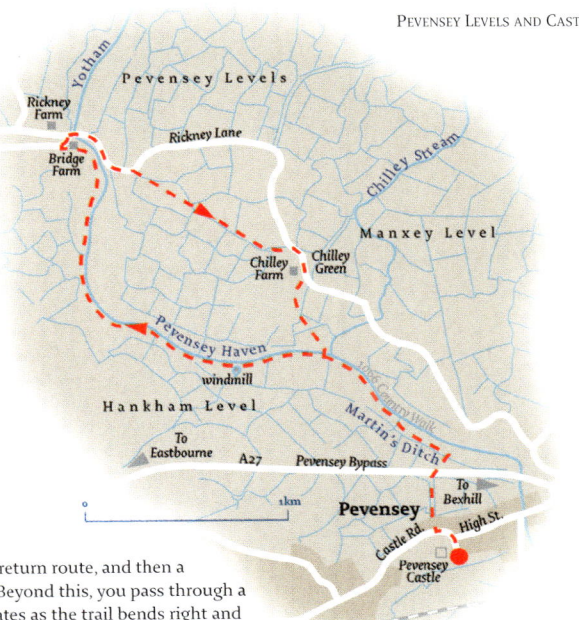

marks the return route, and then a windmill. Beyond this, you pass through a series of gates as the trail bends right and heads northwards to Bridge Farm, where the path leaves Pevensey Haven and passes to the left of the farm to a gate onto a lane. Here, turn right and then right again onto Rickney Lane over Pevensey Haven.

At this point, leave the 1066 Country Walk, which heads off left, and continue down the lane and round the first left-hand bend. At the second left-hand bend, take the footpath off right over a stile. Turn left through a large gate and follow the right of way, which heads southeastwards over the marsh for 400m, with a ditch over on the left, to a footbridge. Continue in the same

direction, now with a ditch on the right, to the higher ground occupied by Chilley Farm, where the footpath crosses a ditch and then heads along a track to Rickney Lane.

Turn right along the lane round the bend and, just past the farm sheds, fork right down the farm track past the buildings. The footpath forks left here and heads over three fields to the footbridge over Pevensey Haven. Across the bridge, turn left and retrace the outward route back beside Pevensey Haven, alongside Martin's Ditch and over the A27 to return to the start.

◀ The inner bailey wall and gatehouse of Pevensey Castle

Alfriston and Windover Hill

Distance 12.5km (incl short detour)
Time 3 hours 30 **Terrain** riverside paths,
woodland and open downland
Map OS Explorer OL25 **Access** bus to
Alfriston from Seaford, Eastbourne
and Hailsham

**Enjoy this classic route over the South
Downs and visit one of the largest areas
of chalk heath in the country.**

The walk starts from the village of
Alfriston, one of the most attractive and
most visited in Sussex. Longer stay
parking is available in The Willows car
park off North Street. Places can be at a
premium at peak periods as many people
come here to visit the Clergy House, a
Wealden 'Hall House' and the first
building to be acquired by the National
Trust in 1896, or St Andrew's Church,

known as the Cathedral of the South
Downs, or just for a wander around the
galleries, cafés, pubs and shops.

In the centre of the village at the top of
the High Street, head down narrow River
Lane on the route of the South Downs
Way and dogleg right, then left across
White Bridge over the Cuckmere River.

Turn right with the South Downs Way
and follow the well-waymarked trail
beside the river. After 1.7km, just beyond a
gate and a right bend, turn left up to the
village of Litlington. Turn right along the
lane past The Plough and Harrow to the
junction at the bend. Dogleg briefly left,
then right to stay on the South Downs
Way, which heads into fields for the next
1km. Climb steeply up the first field and
then along the edges of three more fields
over the rise and down to the edge of
Friston Forest by Charleston Manor.

Turn left and follow the South Downs
Way for another 100m to a path junction.
Fork left off the South Downs Way here
and follow the bridleway which leads

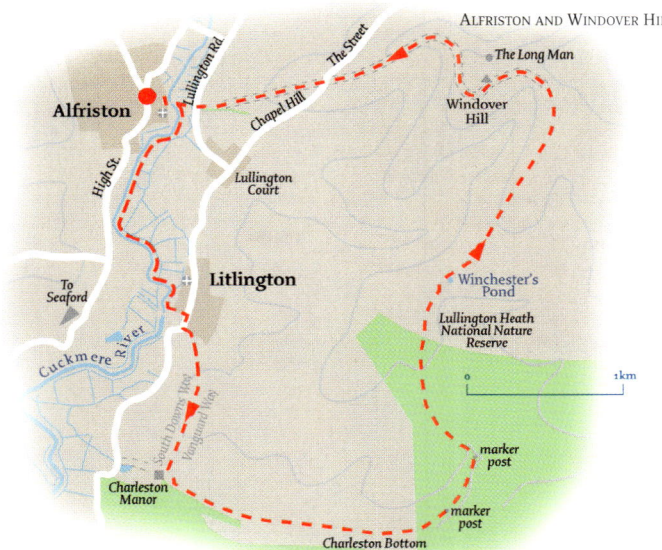

gently up Charleston Bottom. After 1.5km, pass through a gate and continue between stands of woodland over a bridleway crosspaths and up to a marker post just before a gate at a six-track junction.

Turn left and take the bridleway steadily uphill through woodland for 1km to a cross-track at the start of Lullington Heath National Nature Reserve. Keep ahead over the heath for 400m to a bridleway crosspaths. Bear half-right along the track up to the northern edge of the reserve. Continue ahead on the bridleway uphill along the edge of two long fields above Deep Dean. As the bridleway bends left round the head of the dene you join the South Downs Way up to the gate at the top. Turn left with

the South Downs Way over the top of Windover Hill. The highest point and its long barrow lie a little off to the right.

Continue on the South Downs Way, which winds its way down the west side of the hill to a lane. Cross over the lane and continue past the parking area. After 100m, as the track bends right, leave the South Downs Way and fork left onto a footpath down two fields, with the church in Alfriston visible directly ahead. (You can make a short detour off left along the Cuckmere Pilgrim Path to the tiny Church of the Good Shepherd.) At the end of the second field, bear right down to Plonk Barn. Cross over Lullington Road and follow the tarmac walkway back to White Bridge and Alfriston.

◀ St Andrew's Church and The Tye, Alfriston

Eastbourne and the Seven Sisters

Distance 16km **Time** 5 hours (one way)
Terrain seafront promenade and clifftop
paths with a cumulative height gain of
500m **Map** OS Explorer OL25
Access trains to Eastbourne from
Brighton and London Victoria; buses to
Eastbourne from Brighton, Lewes and
Hastings; return from Exceat by bus

**Pack a picnic and stride out along the
South Downs Way from one of Sussex's
most celebrated seaside towns.**

This is a linear walk from Eastbourne
to Exceat via Beachy Head and the Seven
Sisters, which uses the regular coastal
bus service (12) to return from Exceat
to Eastbourne. It would also be possible
to leave a car at the Seven Sisters Visitor
Centre car park at Exceat and take the
bus to the start.

From Eastbourne railway station, head
along the pedestrianised Terminus Road,
signed for the seafront and the pier. At
the seafront, turn right and follow the
promenade alongside Grand Parade for
2km past the town's famous Bandstand,
Wish Tower and giant Wheel. Near the end
of the promenade, by Holywell Chalets,
fork right up Holywell Drive past the
Italian Garden and the Helen Garden.
Continue up to the bend on Duke's Drive
and the junction with the South Downs
Way, whose waymarks are followed over
Beachy Head and the Seven Sisters.

Turn left onto the South Downs Way,
which follows the lower path to Beachy
Head along the cliffs past Whitebread
Hole, now a golfing area, and over the rise
into the next cove before turning right
steeply uphill. At the top, turn left and

◄ On Flagstaff Brow looking back along the route towards Birling Gap

head past a Second World War memorial, where you can take a higher path up to the very top of Beachy Head, with its visitor centre across the road.

For the next 4km, the route heads along the clifftops down to Shooters Bottom before the climb up past Belle Tout Lighthouse, now converted to residential use. From here, you continue down to Birling Gap where there is a National Trust café, toilets and car park.

The South Downs Way heads away from the cliffs and passes to the right of the buildings up a track past bungalows. Just before the last house, make sure you bear left off the track to stay on the South Downs Way. For the next 3km, the route now heads up and down the grassy clifftops of the Seven Sisters. It's easy to lose count but the walking and views keep getting better, and even when it's windy there is some shelter available in the dips.

At the top of Haven Brow, the last Sister, just before the fence, the South Downs Way bears right and descends to Cuckmere Haven at Foxhole. To reach Exceat from here, either continue along the South Downs Way, which forks right up over the remaining spurs on the hillside, or follow the level track beside the river for 1.25km to the Seven Sisters Visitor Centre, where you will find the bus stop at its entrance and the handy Saltmarsh Café.

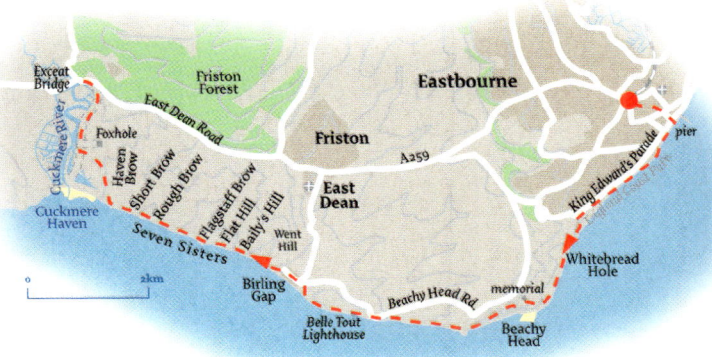

Cuckmere Haven and Seaford Head

Distance 6.75km **Time** 2 hours (one way)
Terrain tracks, cliff edge paths and
seafront esplanade **Map** OS Explorer OL25
Access bus to Seven Sisters Visitor Centre
at Exceat from Seaford and Eastbourne;
trains to Seaford from Lewes; return to
Exceat by bus

**West is best on this less frequented route
for some dramatic views where the South
Downs meet the sea.**

The walk starts from the Seven Sisters
Visitor Centre at Exceat and is accessible
by the regular coastal bus service (12)
between Seaford and Eastbourne. For
those wishing to drive to the start and
return by bus, the visitor centre has a car
park, which can become very busy at peak
periods. The centre also houses the
Saltmarsh Café. The course of the
Cuckmere River as it meanders its way to
the sea at Cuckmere Haven has become
one of the most popular images of this
part of the South Downs and there is now
a level surfaced path on the river's eastern
side. This route reaches Cuckmere Haven
along the track to the west of the river and
then climbs the heights of Seaford Head.

From the Seven Sisters Visitor Centre,
cross the A259 and turn right along the
pedestrian walkway parallel with the road
for 500m to Exceat Bridge. On the far side
of the Cuckmere River, turn left through
the car park of the Cuckmere Inn and
follow signs for the England Coast Path to
Seaford Head. The footpath leads along a
track which starts off close to the river but
soon veers away and passes between
saltmarsh on the left and fields on the
right. The surface is generally good and
initially you share the route with the
National Route 2 cyclepath.

After just over 1km, the track bends left
and rises gently towards the coastguard
cottages at Cuckmere Haven. Here, you
can detour left to the Cable Hut and the

beach for some beachcombing amid the rockpools if the tide is out.

The onward route passes to the right of the coastguard cottages and then follows the England Coast Path along the clifftop, from where there are clear views back to the cliffs of the Seven Sisters and beyond to Beachy Head. Climb over the rise and descend to Hope Bottom and Hope Gap, where you can see large boulders on the beach, the result of frequent cliff fall. The climb from Hope Gap is steep at first but then eases as you pass between fields and the cliff edge, past the aircraft beacon away on the right and then alongside the golf course to the top of Seaford Head.

From the high point there is a good view along the coast over Seaford to Newhaven and Brighton beyond. The walk now descends steeply down beside the golf course to the Esplanade. Follow this past beach huts, the Martello Tower Museum and seafront apartments. After just under 1km, turn right along West View and then head up Pelham Road and Dane Road to the town centre, where you will find the railway station and bus stops on Station Approach, the A259.

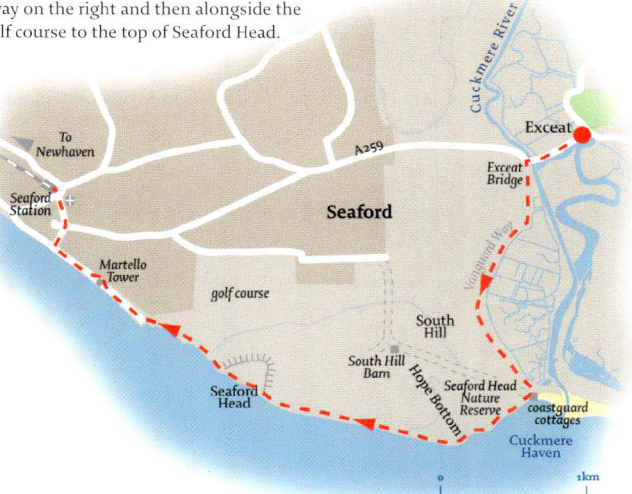

◀ The view eastwards over Cuckmere Haven to Haven Brow

Tenterden

Hawkhurst

Sandhurst

A268

Bodiam 1

Northiam

Robertsbridge

2

A268

Peasmarsh

Rye

3

Sedlescombe

Winchelsea

4

5

Battle

Westfield

Icklesham

Hastings

8

Fairlight
Cove

Bexhill

7

R y e   B a y

Bodiam Castle from the southwest ▶

A259

This part of East Sussex contains many of the most historically significant sites in the South East. Bodiam Castle, with its medieval corner towers, gatehouse and still intact moat, sits majestically on the banks of the River Rother near the border with Kent, while the ruins of Camber Castle near Rye still stand guard over the county's southern approaches, though the sea has long since receded. The Cinque Ports of Winchelsea and Rye both have well-preserved fortifications and are the closest equivalent to continental medieval hilltop towns this side of the Channel. To the west lies the Wealden town of Battle, which takes its name from one of the most famous military engagements in British history. To the south lies the seaside town of Hastings, often seen as far less trendy than its western neighbour Brighton, though Hastings' Old Town and the fishing quarter around The Stade point to the town's longevity and maritime past. To the east of Hastings is a less well-known stretch of coastline, now managed as Hastings Country Park. Its combination of high sandstone cliffs, wooded dells and wildlife-rich heathland make this a dramatic location for walking.

Hastings, Battle and Rye

Bodiam and Udiam

Distance 6.5km (incl detour to Ewhurst Green) **Time** 1 hour 45 **Terrain** riverside paths, lanes, fields and woods
Map OS Explorer 136 **Access** bus to Bodiam from Hawkhurst and Hastings

Amble over the rolling countryside of the Rother Valley with a chance to visit a glorious moated castle.

The walk starts from the National Trust car park for Bodiam Castle at the southern end of Bodiam village. The moated castle dates from the 14th century and even though the interior is now a ruin its massive walls and moat continue to attract many visitors. There is a National Trust café and shop by the car park.

From the car park entrance, head along the walkway parallel with the road over Bodiam Bridge and turn left with the Sussex Border Path alongside the River Rother. The trail follows the raised bank parallel with the river for 350m and then bears right alongside a ditch to the Kent and East Sussex Railway line. Here, dogleg right for just over 100m, then left across the railway track back into fields.

Follow the Sussex Border Path along the right-hand edge of the first field to a path junction just into the second field. The trail bears left through a gate to climb up the third field and alongside a wood in the fourth field, with Ewhurst Place up on the right. Pass through the small wood and head up the right edge of the fifth field to Ewhurst Green. If you want to visit the village centre, you can detour left for 400m past tile-knapped cottages to The Green, the Church of St James the Great and The White Dog Inn.

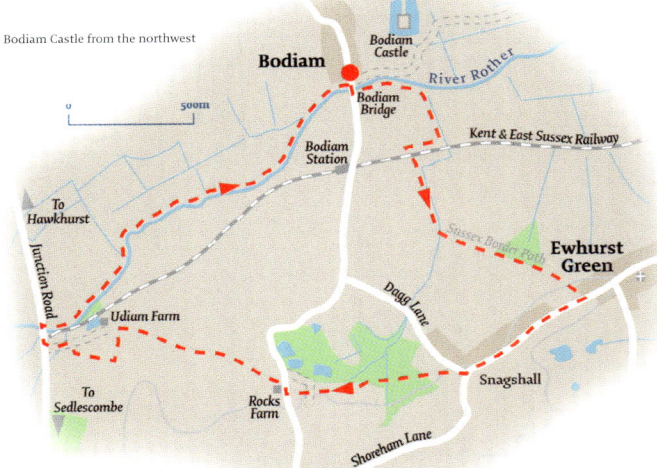

◀ Bodiam Castle from the northwest

The onward route turns right along the pavement past Ewhurst Place and then continues along the narrow lane past the houses of Snagshall to the junction with Dagg Lane. Take the footpath opposite into fields. Head across the first field, then down through woodland and over a footbridge. Continue up through an old orchard to a track, cross over it and head across the bottom of two more fields to the road.

Dogleg right along the road for 30m, then left down past the entrance gate to Rocks Farm. Continue downhill along the left-hand edge of two fields beside a stream and cross over a footbridge and then a second smaller bridge. Just beyond, a quick dogleg left out of the trees and then right takes you up the field edge alongside the wood to a track junction. Take the track ahead to the right of the line of trees down to a driveway. The footpath turns left for 100m up the driveway past the buildings of Udiam Farm and then bears right down the field edge past the former farmhouse. At the bottom, follow the fenced pathway to the driveway, turn left along it for just 50m and then fork right to a small gate in the hedge onto Junction Road.

At the road, the route turns right along the narrow grass verge for 100m and, across the River Rother, heads off right onto the winding waterside path for the final 1.75km back to Bodiam Bridge.

Peasmarsh and Iden

Distance 8km **Time** 2 hours 15
Terrain lanes, orchards, fields and
woodland **Map** OS Explorer 125 **Access** bus
to Peasmarsh from Rye and Northiam

**Enjoy a leisurely stroll between two
villages through orchards and past a
medieval moated farmhouse.**

The walk starts towards the western
end of Peasmarsh, 150m up from the
Memorial Hall. There is a car park for
Jempson's Supermarket (closed on
Sundays) on Tanhouse Lane at the
western end of the village or parking is
possible on residential roads off Main
Street, the A268. Head down the bridleway
along the lane signed for Forstals Farm
and Old House Farm. The lane descends
gently between fields and then through
woodland for 700m to the entrance to
Old House Farm.

Pass between the house and the farm
buildings and continue down the
bridleway which heads along a track
between fields and then bears left up to a
path junction. Turn right along the edge
of a vineyard and then fork left with the
bridleway through orchards to the
buildings of Moat Farm. This site dates
back to medieval times and when
constructed in the 14th century would
have been protected by its moat from
raiders and animals. Access would have
been along causeways and there may even
have been a wharf for landing cargoes.

At the farmhouse, bend right and
follow the driveway which winds its way
up to the farm buildings at Readers Lane.
Turn right up the lane for 100m and then
follow the footpath off left into an
orchard. The footpath heads diagonally
past an electricity pylon through the

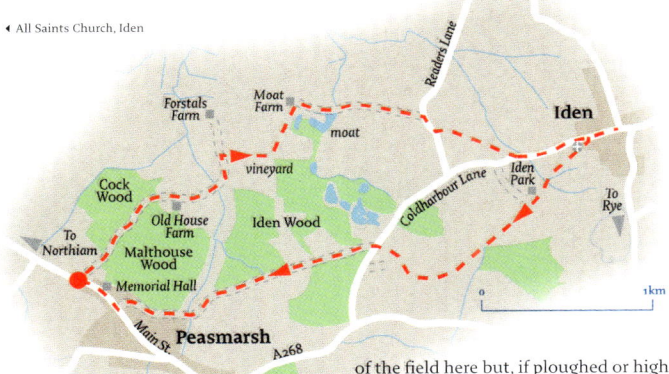

◀ All Saints Church, Iden

middle of the orchard to Coldharbour Lane. Turn left and follow the narrow lane up into the village of Iden to All Saints Church. The centre of the village with its village stores lies 150m further on.

The return route turns right opposite Park Cottage to the church. It's a delightfully simple church and inside is a painting of *The Prodigal Son* by Hans Feibusch. Continue past the church and across the recreation ground, where the footpath heads past the pavilion and through trees into fields. Follow the right-hand edge of the first field past Iden Park House, cross over a bridleway and continue over the next field past a dell with a small lake. Aim for the bottom left corner and cross into a large third field.

The right of way cuts across the bottom of the field here but, if ploughed or high with crops, follow the field edge down to the corner and up to the right for 150m. The right of way now technically crosses to the other side of the fence for the next 100m before crossing back over and continuing up the field edge to the top by some farm buildings. Here, bear right across a fourth field and then left along the edge of the fifth to Coldharbour Lane.

The route now doglegs left along the lane and almost immediately right onto the byway to the left of the track to Idenwood Farm. The byway, which is closed to motor vehicles, heads through woodland for 1km over a slight rise and down to a gate. Bend left with the byway down to the recreation ground on the edge of Peasmarsh and continue to follow it gently uphill along the backs of houses, where it narrows to a path and bends left to the A268 Rye Road just down from the Memorial Hall.

Sedlescombe and Ward's Wood

Distance 7km **Time** 2 hours
Terrain lanes, fields and woodland
Map OS Explorer 124 **Access** bus to
Sedlescombe from Hawkhurst
and Hastings

**Follow a now tranquil route over fields
and through woods with a hidden
industrial past.**

Sedlescombe is an attractive village
alongside the B2244. On The Green is the
old parish pump covered by a Victorian
well-house and surrounded by timber,
brick and tile-hung houses, the oldest
dating from the 15th century. At the
southern edge of the village, the River
Brede flows quietly under the bridge.
All seems a rural idyll, but on the route
you pass Powdermill Reservoir. Its name
is a reminder that gunpowder used to be
produced here and in 1764 a powder mill
at the bottom of the village blew up with
devastating effect.

The walk starts from The Green and

there is parking alongside The Street or in
the council car park nearby on Brede Lane.
Walk up The Street, the B2244, for 200m
and, opposite Roselands Drive, turn right
onto a footpath up a track past houses.
Continue up past Red Barn Field Nature
Park to a gate. The route now continues
gently uphill along the edges of four
fields, with a fine view left across the
valley to Sedlescombe Church.

At the top by Killingan Wood, go
through the gate and fork right up
Churchland Lane. After 200m, opposite a
house called Woodstock, make sure you
fork left, off the rough lane, to continue
on the footpath along the edge of
Killingan Wood and then down between
gardens to Hurst Lane. Cross the lane and
keep on down through trees, signed for
Powdermill Reservoir, to a gate into fields.
The footpath continues beside a line of
oak trees and then down over the field to
the gate at the bottom.

Keep on down into Brede Woods along a

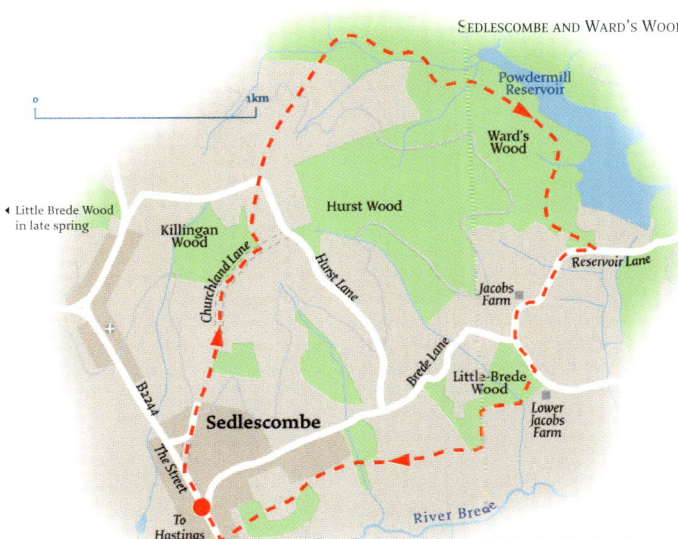

0   1km

◄ Little Brede Wood
in late spring

Powdermill
Reservoir

Ward's
Wood

Killingan
Wood

Hurst Wood

Reservoir Lane

Churchland Lane

Hurst Lane

Jacobs
Farm

B2244

Brede Lane

Little Brede
Wood

Sedlescombe

Lower
Jacobs
Farm

The Street

To
Hastings

River Brede

track over a stream and, after another 50m, at the path junction turn right. Follow the footpath beside the stream for 400m to a footbridge. The footpath crosses the bridge and heads up away from the stream on an undulating path through the mixed woodland of Ward's Wood. After 800m, the path bends right and then crosses two more footbridges near the southern end of Powdermill Reservoir, visible off to the left through the trees. Keep on through the woodland and follow the footpath as it bends left down to Reservoir Lane.

The onward route turns right up the winding lane past the entrance to Jacobs Farm and down to a junction. Fork left along Brede Lane for 200m and, just

before the end of Little Brede Wood, turn right along a narrow fenced footpath down to a stile into fields. Turn right along the edge of the field to the corner and continue round to the left for another 150m. At this point, make sure you bear right with the footpath through the southern tip of the wood to a footbridge and stile into a second field.

The route now follows the right-hand edge of a series of fields. In the fourth field, by the end of the houses, cross a stile and continue along a short fenced section into a fifth field. Head along the field edge to a gate into woodland and a path junction. Follow the right fork through the trees and then continue down past gardens and houses to the B2244, where a right turn will take you back up to The Green in Sedlescombe.

85

Rye and Camber Castle

Distance 6km **Time** 1 hour 30
Terrain town streets, fields and
marshland (muddy and prone to
flooding in wet conditions)
Map OS Explorer 125 **Access** trains to
Rye from Hastings and Ashford; bus
to Rye from Hastings

**This walk is full of history and starts
from one of the best surviving examples
of a medieval hilltop town.**

There is no shortage of attractions that
draw visitors to the ancient fortified town
of Rye – the cobbled streets, the medieval
walls and town gates, the town's links
with the Confederation of the Cinque
Ports, the Ypres Tower and museum, the
Norman St Mary's Church, the novelist
Henry James's former home of Lamb
House, the connection with the artist
Paul Nash, the Royal Military Canal, the
yachts moored on Strand Quay. However,

on the marshes outside the town lies the
far less frequented Camber Castle. This
was built in the early 16th century on
what was then a long shingle ridge
overlooking Rye Harbour. Henry VIII soon
had it enlarged to counter the threat of a
French invasion, but a century later
during the Civil War the castle was
partially dismantled. Today, the
substantial ruin stands in eerie isolation.

From the railway station, head up
Station Approach past the bus stops and
turn right along Cinque Ports Street. Keep
straight on at the traffic island, then curve
right down Wish Street to Strand Quay
and keep ahead onto Winchelsea Road. If
starting from the town centre, walk along
the High Street, turn right down Market
Road and then turn left onto Cinque Ports
Street opposite Station Approach. Long-
stay parking is available on the west side
of the town at Gibbet Marsh car park.

From here, take the path out of the back of the car park towards Rye Windmill, bear right over the railway and then alongside the River Tillingham to Strand Quay. Turn right onto Winchelsea Road.

The route heads along the pavement of Winchelsea Road for 400m, turns left along Harbour Road and crosses the canal by Brede Lock at the bend. Here, keep ahead onto a footpath through light woodland to a gate onto the marshland of Castle Water Nature Reserve, with Camber Castle visible off to the right. Continue along the raised path for 600m over two fields to some buildings and a small patch of woodland. Head through the woodland and over a small footbridge. At the fork in the path beyond, bear right and follow the fence to a gate. Bear a little right and follow the path around the northern side of Castle Water. After a third gate by a ditch the footpath bears left across the large field towards Camber Castle.

The return route heads to the right of the castle to the fence. Turn right and follow the footpath beside the fence along a grassy track for 400m to a gateway. Go through the gate and join the bridleway which carries the Royal Military Canal Path. From here, the route heads alongside a ditch and then bends round to the right to reach a gate by the canal. Go through the gate and fork left to continue beside the canal. After 250m, go past some willow trees to a gate, continue along the footpath past Castle Mill Cottages and bear left down the driveway to Brede Lock. From here, turn left and retrace your steps along Winchelsea Road to the centre of Rye

◄ The ruins of Camber Castle

Winchelsea and Icklesham

Distance 8km **Time** 2 hours 15
Terrain lanes, fields and marshland
Map OS Explorer 124 **Access** bus to
Winchelsea from Rye and Hastings;
trains from Hastings and Ashford to
Winchelsea Station, located north of the
town, 2km along the 1066 Country Walk

**Enjoy the perfect combination of town
and country on this route from one of
the ancient Cinque Ports.**

Winchelsea is a rare example of a
medieval planned town and is often
referred to as New Winchelsea to
distinguish it from the original
settlement which was swept away by a
series of vicious storms in the 13th
century. The new town was built on the
higher ground of Iham Hill and laid out
in a grid pattern. On the walk you pass
the town ditch and New Gate which now
stand isolated in fields and give a sense
of how large the town once was.

From the centre of Winchelsea by
St Thomas' Church, head down the
pavement of Monk's Walk on the route of
the 1066 Country Walk, which is well-
waymarked and followed to Icklesham.
Go round the bend past the ruined wall of
St John's Hospital and bear left down two
fields to a gate by the town ditch, where
you will see New Gate off to the left. The
1066 Country Walk forks right up the field
past Wickham Manor and over its
driveway. Continue over two more fields,
bear left over Wickham Rock Lane and
head up the next field to a pillbox at the
top of the rise. Continue down two more
fields to the lane again. Dogleg left past
Windmill Cottage, then bear right into
fields, uphill past the former windmill
and back down to Workhouse Lane.

Head round the bend for 50m where a
fingerpost shows the way off right

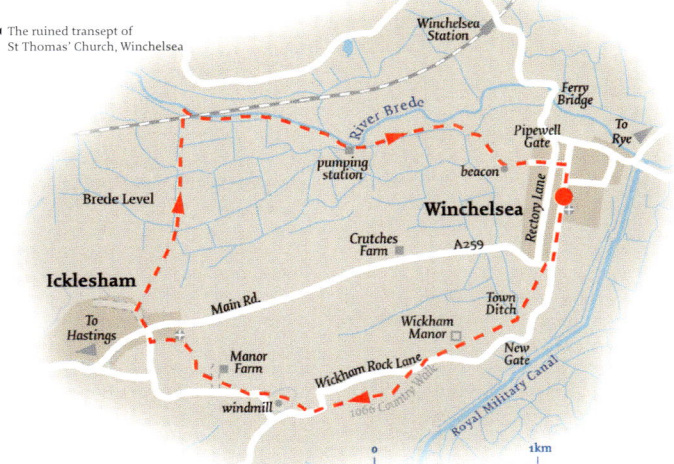

◄ The ruined transept of
St Thomas' Church, Winchelsea

*Winchelsea
Station*

*Ferry
Bridge*

*Pipewell
Gate*

*To
Rye*

River Brede

*pumping
station*

beacon

Winchelsea

Rectory Lane

Brede Level

*Crutches
Farm*

A259

Icklesham

Main Rd.

*Town
Ditch*

*To
Hastings*

*Wickham
Manor*

*New
Gate*

*Manor
Farm*

Wickham Rock Lane

windmill

1066 Country Walk

Royal Military Canal

0   1km

through a gap in the hedge, along a short fenced section and then a field edge to the driveway to Manor Farm Oast. Turn right onto the driveway and then at a marker post before the bend, fork left onto a fenced footpath which follows the field edge round to the left past All Saints and St Nicolas Church to Workhouse Lane at the edge of Icklesham.

Turn right down the lane, cross the A259 and continue along Parsonage Lane to The Queens Head. The route now leaves the 1066 Country Walk and forks right past the pub. At the rear of its car park, take the footpath into fields and head downhill to the low-lying land of the Brede Valley. At the bottom, go through a gate and continue along the footpath on the right of a drain over four fields to the railway line.

The route crosses the railway and then a footbridge over a drain before turning right along the bank of the River Brede and, in 50m, crossing back over the railway. The footpath continues along the steep-banked river for the next 800m to Icklesham Pumping Station. Keep on along the grassy track beyond, now a little away from the river, and after another 700m bear right over two drains to a footpath junction below the escarpment of Iham Hill, on which Winchelsea stands.

Fork right and climb the grassy bank ahead up to the triangulation pillar and beacon at the top, where a topograph points out the features. Continue over the field and cross the A259 just up from Pipewell Gate. To return to the centre of Winchelsea, keep ahead along Mill Road and take the first right back up to St Thomas' Church.

Battle to Crowhurst

Distance 6.5km **Time** 1 hour 45 (one way)
Terrain fields, woodland and lanes
Map OS Explorer 124 **Access** trains to
**Battle and Crowhurst from Hastings and
Royal Tunbridge Wells; bus to Battle from
Hastings and Royal Tunbridge Wells**

**Head off along the easy-to-follow 1066
Country Walk from one of the most
historic sites in England.**

This is a linear walk which starts from
Battle Station. Parking is available at both
Battle and Crowhurst Stations. From the
front of the railway station, turn left up
Station Approach to Lower Lake road, the
A2100, and turn right along the pavement.
At the mini-roundabout, fork left along
Upper Lake road to Abbey Green and
Battle Abbey. Both the town and the
abbey take their name from perhaps

the most well-known event in British
history. William, Duke of Normandy,
founded the abbey here in atonement for
the blood which was shed at the Battle of
Hastings and within the abbey's grounds
is the battlefield site itself, now managed
by English Heritage.

The route follows the 1066 Country
Walk across the front of Battle Abbey and
down Park Lane to the gate into George
Meadow. Head down the left side of the
meadow, through woodland and up to a
path junction and marker post. The 1066
Country Walk splits here. The right fork
heads for Pevensey, but the onward route

takes the left branch on the Bexhill Link, leading alongside woodland and down the field edge to a stream. Continue up the far slope just before the B2095. Cross the track, bear right along the path parallel to and above the road down to the bend and cross the road. Some care is required when crossing.

Head along Telham Lane opposite for 100m and then fork right onto the bridleway along the driveway to Peppering Eye Farm. Continue past the farmhouse and its buildings and join the lane which heads over a rise, down over a stream and uphill again to a path junction by Powdermill Cottage. Turn left with the 1066 Country Walk along the driveway to The Pump House and at the bottom of Stumblet's Wood make sure you turn left over a field to Fore Wood.

The 1066 Country Walk crosses a footbridge, passes through a gate and follows the undulating footpath for just under 1km through Fore Wood Nature Reserve to its far edge. Continue over a field, up through a patch of woodland and then over a second field to the edge of Crowhurst. Bear right along the pavement and keep on round the bend past the school and the Church of St George, which has an ancient yew tree near its south porch, with the remains of a 13th-century Manor House visible just below the churchyard. From the lower entrance to the church, cross to and follow Station Road for 600m to Crowhurst Station.

◄ The entrance to Battle Abbey

Hastings Country Park

Distance 4.5km **Time** 1 hour 30
Terrain a mix of coastal grassland,
heathland and woodland, with some
steep gradients **Map** OS Explorer 124
Access bus to The Bale House Visitor
Centre from Hastings and Rye

**Explore a dramatic maritime country
park with views along the coast and over
the Channel to France.**

The walk starts from The Bale House
Visitor Centre in Hastings Country Park,
where there is a large car park and a café.
The park is a Local Nature Reserve and in
Sussex is a unique combination of sea-
cliffs, heathland, woodland and grassland.
The reserve is located between the seaside
town of Hastings and the settlement of
Fairlight. This walk ranges over the
eastern area of the country park between
Fairlight Glen and Firehills.

From the innovative, energy efficient
and low-carbon visitor centre, which has
been built using load-bearing straw bales,
walk down the surfaced track past the
lower car park to the radar station. The
route bears right below the radar mast
and takes the lower path past post 24
through a gate downhill. The path
descends steeply and then bears right to
post 22. Fork left down the steps here and
continue to post 21 by the stream in the
bottom of Warren Glen.

You now climb steeply up the far side to
a gate and path junction by post 18. Keep
on up the steps through the woodland on
Brakey Bank to the top of the rise and
Lovers' Seat viewpoint. Continue down to
post 17 in Glen Wood. Here, the route
forks right gently uphill, over a stream
and round to the left to the head of
Fairlight Glen. Cross over the stream and

◄ In the western part of Hastings Country Park

head round the left bend to post 15. Make sure you fork right up out of the woodland here and then head alongside a field to a gate and post 13. Continue down the track beyond and bend right up to Barley Lane and post 11.

The route now turns right up the surfaced lane for just over 300m to the bend by the entrance to Fairlight Place. Continue ahead onto a footpath, signed for the visitor centre, for the next 600m along the edge of a wood with fields on the left to a path junction at post 19. Keep ahead and go just past Little Warren Cottage to post 20. Fork left here and follow the path through the disused quarry, where there is an information panel explaining its history. On the far side, go up some narrow steps cut through one of the outcrops and then fork left up to a track, which will take you back to the visitor centre and the start.

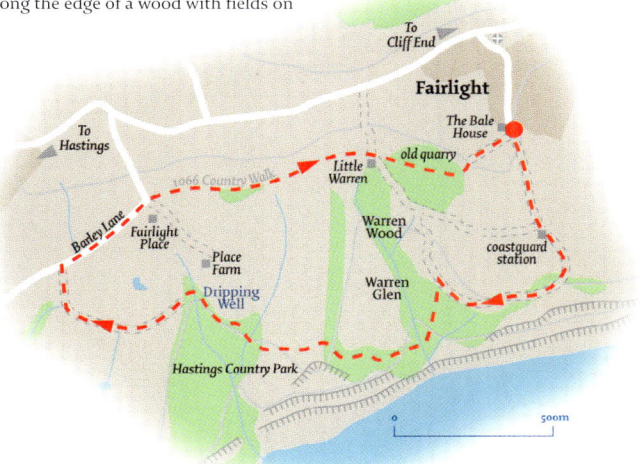

Hastings to Winchelsea

Distance 16km (incl short detour
to visitor centre) **Time** 5 hours (one way)
Terrain promenade, clifftop paths with
some steep gradients and canal path
Map OS Explorer 124 **Access** trains to
Hastings from Eastbourne and Ashford;
bus to Hastings from Eastbourne and Rye

**Stride out along the Saxon Shore Way
from seaside Hastings to medieval
Winchelsea, returning by bus.**

This is a linear walk and starts from the
railway station in Hastings. There is a
regular bus service from Winchelsea back
to Hastings. Alternatively, Winchelsea's
railway station lies to the north of the
town, 2km along the waymarked 1066
Country Walk.

From the station, walk down Havelock
Road to the bottom and bear left through
Wellington Place to the seafront. Turn left
along the promenade to The Stade with
its fishing boats, where you'll find Old
Town off to the left. By Hastings
Contemporary, cross Rock-A-Nore Road

and, just before The Dolphin Inn, turn
left up Tamarisk Steps, signed for East
Hill. A dogleg left along Tackleway and
then right takes you up more steps into
Hastings Country Park to the top of East
Hill. From here, the Saxon Shore Way is
followed until near the end of the walk.

Head down the far side of East Hill into
wooded Ecclesbourne Glen and continue
up the other side. The path bends right
and then back up to the left beside the
fence on Ecclesbourne Meadow before
descending and forking right at post 12
down through Covehurst Wood to the
bottom of Fairlight Glen. The path now
zigzags its way up to a path junction at
post 17. Make sure you fork right up steps,
over the rise of Lovers' Seat and then
steeply down to the bottom of Warren
Glen. Cross the stream and bear left up
through trees to post 22. From here,

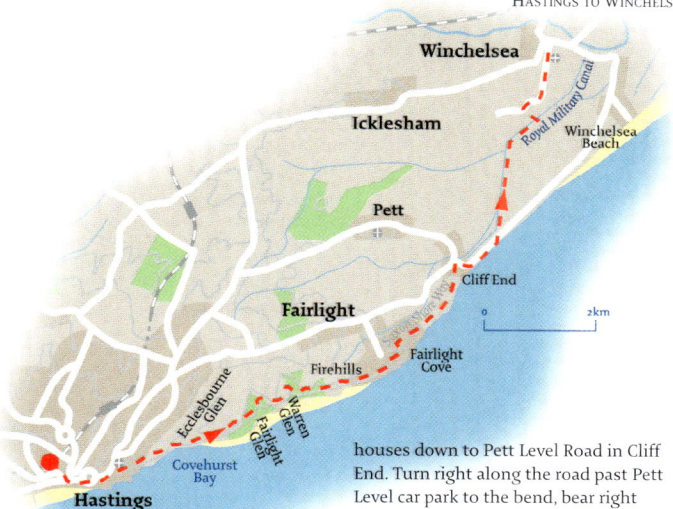

zigzag right, then left up to post 24 by Fairlight Radar Station, where you can detour left up to The Bale House Visitor Centre and café.

The Saxon Shore Way now follows a line below the top of Firehills to the eastern end of the country park and continues down a track past houses on the western edge of Fairlight Cove. Take the second left down Shepherds Way, then right along Bramble Way to the end and left down Smugglers Way. At the bottom, bear right and follow Lower Waites Lane past houses down to a lane junction.

Cross over into a field and turn right onto a footpath which zigzags round a house and then heads up cliffs and along ' wooded section before descending past

houses down to Pett Level Road in Cliff End. Turn right along the road past Pett Level car park to the bend, bear right along a driveway and almost immediately fork left along a footpath to the beach.

Turn left along the seafront to the end of the promenade. Keep on for another 100m, descend the second set of steps, cross the road and head along a track to the canal. The route now turns right alongside the Royal Military Canal over Pett Level. After just under 2km, you pass a footbridge and the canal bends to the right. Continue for another 500m to a second footbridge and turn left, off the Saxon Shore Way, across the canal, over the marshy field beyond and up to Wickham Rock Lane. The final part of the route turns right along the lane down past New Gate Cottages and then uphill through New Gate to the junction with Monks' Walk. Continue ahead here up the pavement to the centre of Winchelsea.

Index